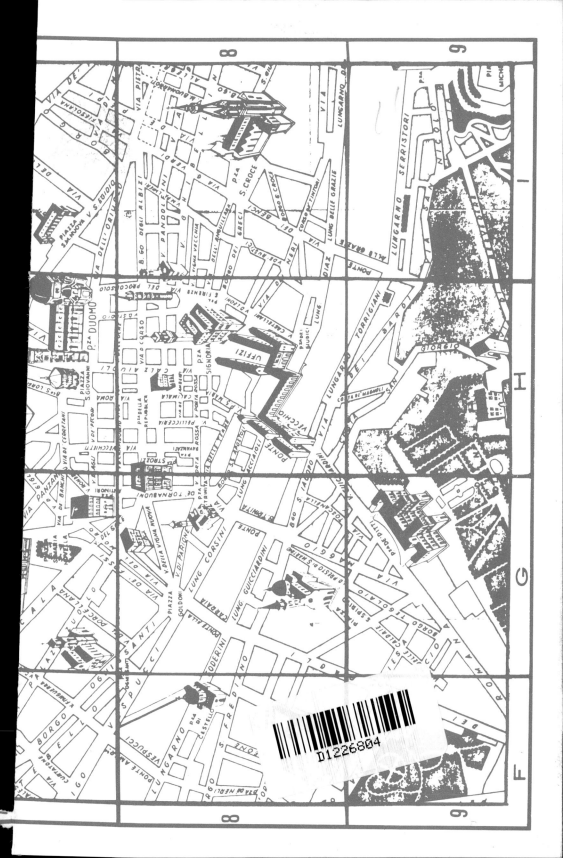

ART AND ARCHITECTURE
IN THE POETRY
OF ROBERT BROWNING
APPENDIX A

ART AND ARCHITECTURE IN THE POETRY OF ROBERT BROWNING APPENDIX A

An Illustrated Compendium of Sources

Charles Flint Thomas

The Whitston Publishing Company
Troy, New York
1996

Library of Congress Catalog Card Number 87-50834

ISBN 0-87875-467-9

Printed in the United States of America

In memory of my dear mother,
Mrs. John Harold Thomas,
formerly Grace Helen Lewis,
and Mrs. Crawford Burbank Waterman,
and dedicated to my good father,
Mr. John Harold Thomas.

Frontispiece
Henry Alfred Pegram
Elizabeth Barrett Browning
South London Art Gallery
(see the Introduction to the *Compendium*
and THOMA under the
Key to Bibliography in this appendix)

CONTENTS

NOTICE

Essential to an understanding of the scope of this study are the overviews in the Preface and Introduction to *Appendix A*. Readers who are in contact with the *Compendium* for the first time are advised to proceed directly to these overviews before looking into the individual entries in the *Compendium* and *Appendix A*.

In addition, *Appendix B* to the *Compendium* is in current preparation. Readers who wish to submit contributions for *Appendix B*, revisions or corrections for *Appendix A*, and inquiries to the author are sincerely invited to send them to the following address:

Notes & Queries
Studies in Browning and His Circle
Baylor University
P. O. Box 97152
Waco, TX 76798-7152

PREFACE

Appendix A clarifies, updates, supplements, revises, and corrects *Art and Architecture in the Poetry of Robert Browning: An Illustrated Compendium of Sources. Appendix A* is designed after and is to be used in conjunction with the *Compendium*. Clarification of the *Compendium* is primarily assigned in *Appendix A* to the Introduction; updating and supplementation to the Citations and Notes, and to the Illustrations; and revision and correction are placed in a new section titled Corrections and Revisions. The Introduction has overarching scope: it covers a review of the foundation studies leading up to the *Compendium* and *Appendix A*, definitions of terms, and a statement of significance for the whole study. The Citations and Notes contain supplementary material that adds to or comments on the sources and analyses given in the *Compendium*. The Illustrations continue from the numbering in the *Compendium*. End sections also clarify, update, supplement, revise, and correct the *Compendium*. These end sections are, in addition to the Corrections and Revisions, the Chronology, the Summary of Composite Sources, the Index of Artists, the Index of Sources with Locations, the Index of Miscellaneous Sources, the Key to Bibliography, and the maps of Florence and Rome.

The updating and supplementing of the citations, notes, and illustrations further enrich the content of this study. The additional sources entered in *Appendix A* number about 60; some 35 of these, I would say, are being introduced into Browning studies for the first time. The total number of analyses in *Appendix A* amounts to about 40; the vast portion of these, I surmise, is fresh. Of special novelty and interest in *Appendix A* are the source studies and analyses of pictures, sculpture, and architecture entered under *Christmas-Eve and Easter-Day*, "Cleon," "Eurydice to Orpheus," *Fifine at the Fair*, "Flute-Music, with an Accompaniment," "A Grammarian's Funeral," "Inapprehensiveness," "My Last Duchess" in conjunction with *Pippa*

Passes, "Parleying with Francis Furini," "Parleying with Gerard de Lairesse," and *The Ring and the Book.* An abundance of the new material may be found under "Parleying with Gerard de Lairesse."

ACKNOWLEDGMENTS

Gratitude is extended to my readers, Professors Collmer, DeLaura, Eisenberg, Herring, and Ormond, whose expertise and contributions are set forth in the Preface and Acknowledgments to the *Compendium* and, in the cases of Professors DeLaura and Eisenberg, in the Key to Bibliography below under DELAU and EISE. All of these individuals are still actively teaching and doing research, although Professors Collmer and DeLaura have stepped down from their administrative positions, and Professor Eisenberg is now emeritus from the University of Michigan. The rereading of this study by these scholars after a hiatus of several years has resulted in many helpful suggestions and is indicative of their continued support and encouragement. Others most helpful and supportive are Professor Roger L. Brooks, Director of the Armstrong Browning Library, and staff librarians, Mrs. Cynthia A. Burgess, Mrs. Betty A. Coley, and Mrs. Rita S. Humphrey. Finally, my thanks are expressed to Mr. Kalle Valdma, photographer and researcher, for his very important assistance; to Mrs. Jean Goode, President of the Whitston Publishing Company, for her patience and tolerance in accepting the interminable changes and additions to this study; to Fukuoka Jo Gakuin College for funds to help finance the color photography in this appendix; and to Mr. Michael Meredith, Librarian of Eton College, for special consultation on particular poems.

Numerous institutions are acknowledged here for providing photographic services for this appendix. In parentheses after the names of the institutions are the figure numbers for the illustrations. Illustrations that are not listed here have been provided by Mr. Valdma and myself. In the *Compendium*, pages xi and xii, special forms acknowledging "permission" and "courtesy" have been given that are required by some institutions. Of the entries below only the last one requires a special form of acknowledgment.

Photographic Credits:

Academy of Fine Arts, Budapest (Fig. 284)

Archeological Museum, Naples (Fig. 297)

Armstrong Browning Library, Waco (Figs. 286, 289, from photographs; originals in private collections)

Azienda di Turismo, Bolzano (Fig. 276)

Azienda di Turismo, Varallo (Fig. 298)

Court Church, Innsbruck (Figs. 292, 293)

Elmer Belt Library of Vinciana, University of California, Los Angeles (Figs. 277, 290, 291)

Gabinetto Fotografico, Soprintendenza alle Gallerie, Florence (Figs. 262, 264, 265, 266, 267, 279, 280, 281, 285, 296)

Gabinetto Fotografico, Nazionale, Rome (Figs. 272, 300)

Hohen-Schwangau Castle, Füssen, Germany (Fig. 294)

Manchester City Art Gallery (Fig. 274)

Museo di Capodimonte (National Museum), Naples (Fig. 263)

National Gallery, London (Fig. 283)

National Museum of Villa Giulia, Rome (Fig. 261)

National Portrait Gallery, London (Fig. 275, from a photograph; original in private collection)

Naval Museum, Venice (Fig. 299)

Princeton University Art Museum (Fig. 282)

South London Art Gallery (Frontispiece)

Trask Family Estate, Saratoga Springs (Yaddo Foundation) (Fig. 287)

Vatican Museums (Fig. 278)

Villa Medicea, Poggio a Caiano (Figs. 268, 269)

Wellesley College, reproduction courtesy of Clapp Library, Special Collections (Fig. 288)

INTRODUCTION

In retrospect, now that the *Compendium* is published, it is impressed upon me that this study stands to gain from more background, clarity, and generalized points of significance. Accordingly, I will review three foundation works, define four terms, and make a statement of the overall importance of the study. The foundation works are Ph.D. dissertations by Conroy, Alberti, and myself. The four terms to be defined are the words "real," "unspecified," "imaginary," and "composite" as applied to Browning's use of sources for pictures, sculpture, and architecture. The significance of this study attaches to its value as a repository for and guide to art history, a storehouse of literary images and symbolism, a possible unravelling of Browning's creative method, a basis for future research, and a claim for Browning's place in literature as the most pictorial, sculptural, and architectural of all poets, that is, as the universally supreme poet in the use of painting, sculpture, and architecture.

In 1971, Marilyn Ann Conroy's dissertation, "Browning's Use of Art Objects," appeared (CON). It was the first study not only to cover Browning's education in art history but also to give a sampling of the sources for the art and architecture in his poetry and to establish a rationale for the analysis of his use of art and architecture. Conroy's coverage of Browning's education in art history is summarized in the *Compendium* and this appendix under the sections titled Chronology. Conroy's sampling of sources for art and architecture entails about 70 citations, some 55 of which are descriptive of painting, 10 of sculpture, and 5 of architecture. Although Conroy's sampling of sources is not original, it is diverse and covers about 40 poems that span Browning's early, middle, and late periods. Conroy concludes that art and architecture in Browning's poetry embody the infinite within the finite. Pictures, sculpture, and architecture are not mere decoration for Browning's poetry. They are concerned with what may be termed their metaphorical, emblematic, or symbolic meaning, with what Conroy calls "a metaphor not only for poetry but also for the perceptual and epistemological—the judgmental—processes in which we all engage" (CON, 177).

The next foundation study of Browning's use of art and architecture is Judith Fay Alberti's 1979 dissertation, "Robert Browning and Italian Renaissance Painting" (AL). This work focuses on poems of the early and middle periods that describe Italian Renaissance painting, with particular emphasis on "Andrea del Sarto," "Fra Lippo Lippi," and "Old Pictures in Florence." Background material on Browning's preparation in art history is also included, with special attention to Vasari's *Lives*. Alberti's attributions of sources, although limited almost exclusively to Italian Renaissance painting up through the *Men and Women* poems, are copious and, in many cases, original, particularly in reference to sources from Vasari. She includes thirty-eight illustrations, some of which are unusual. About two dozen of her ideas that I consider unique are recorded in the *Compendium* and this appendix; they are summarized almost solely under the three great painter poems listed above. Alberti's analysis of painting is rich and complex. She makes it clear that painting as metaphor—or emblem or symbol—is indeed, as Conroy advocates, the putting of infinite meaning into finite form, and she moves on to demonstrate that Browning's symbolism leads to his major themes, especially the Doctrine of the Imperfect and the related theme of Browning's preference for Christian art to Greco-Roman art.

My own dissertation, "Robert Browning's Poetic Art Objects: An Illustrated Compendium" (THOMAS), also appeared in 1979. It was an effort to expand Conroy's study by being more comprehensive and detailed, yet it was also analytical. After I became aware of the originality of Alberti's work, I combined comprehensiveness and detail with an expanded identification of sources so that by the time I published the *Compendium* twelve years after the dissertation, and now *Appendix A* five years after the *Compendium*, I had brought the total number of poems to over 80, the illustrations to over 300, the total number of sources to about 560, and the amount of presumed original sources to about 135 out of the total number of sources. Because of the amassing of new data, the format of a reference book was adopted and analysis was subordinated to source study. This appendix, however, has much more analysis than the *Compendium*, both in quantity and in elaboration, and the projected

Appendix B also should have a large amount of extended criticism. To date, from the *Compendium* through *Appendix A*, the critical comments total about 65. The poems in which the analyses are the most developed are listed above in paragraph two of the Preface.

Increasingly apparent is Browning's use of art and architecture to embody all of his themes: the Doctrine of the Imperfect, in "Andrea del Sarto," "A Grammarian's Funeral," and "Old Pictures in Florence"; the Infinite Moment, in "By the Fireside," and the missed good moment, in "Inapprehensiveness"; a satire of historical personages, such as Napoleon III in *Prince Hohenstiel-Schwangau*, and John Horsley in "Parleying with Francis Furini"; a criticism of Roman Catholicism, in *Christmas-Eve and Easter-Day*, *Prince Hohenstiel-Schwangau*, and *The Ring and the Book*; a characterization of the Italian Renaissance, in "Andrea del Sarto," "The Bishop Orders His Tomb at Saint Praxed's Church," "Fra Lippo Lippi," "My Last Duchess," and "Old Pictures in Florence"; sympathy with the Risorgimento, in "Eurydice to Orpheus," and "Old Pictures in Florence"; the heroic life through rescue and/or quest, in "Childe Roland to the Dark Tower Came," "How They Brought the Good News from Ghent to Aix," and *The Ring and the Book*; and, though I could add more, memorials to Elizabeth Barrett Browning, in *Balaustion's Adventure*, "The Englishman in Italy," "Eurydice to Orpheus," "Flute-Music, with an Accompaniment," "One Word More," and "Prospice."

The first of the four terms that need to be defined is the word "real." Real art and architecture are based on the actual, that which can be found in the body of art and architectural history, or literature and treatises describing art and architecture. Real art and architecture are either referred to or alluded to in Browning's poetry. References operate on a one-to-one basis, that is, for each reference to art and/or architecture, there is one primary source. For example, the Laocoön group sculptures in the Vatican—both the Greek original and the Roman copy—are explicitly referred to in the *Prince Hohenstiel-Schwangau* poem. This is a one-to-one connection with a primary source and its dependence on two real pieces of sculpture.

Allusions to real art and architecture are what I categorize as "unspecified"; they are implicit, not explicit. Allusions to unspecified art and architecture sometimes lend themselves to a number of real sources. For instance, in "Fra Lippo Lippi" the phrase "Giotto, with his Saint a-praising God" could entail many of the pictures of St. Francis attributed to Giotto in the Upper Church and the Lower Church of San Francesco, in Assisi; the number of possible pictures is limited by defining "Saint a-praising God" as St. Francis praying to or preaching about God. In short, this allusion to the work of Giotto is based on an unspecified combination of real sources.

Art and architecture based on mental constructs that are not found in the body of the history of art and architecture or literature and treatises describing art and architecture are what I call "imaginary." Many times imaginary art and architecture in Browning's poetry are not formulated from a single mental construct but from a combination of real sources. Combination sources are conflations, collateral sources, or what I more commonly term "composites." For example, in "Andrea del Sarto" the four great walls in the New Jerusalem are to be painted on or decorated with work by Leonardo da Vinci, Michelangelo, Raphael, and Andrea del Sarto himself. All of these elements together form an imaginary or mental construct; as a total image it does not exist. But the components of the image are not imaginary. Models for the New Jerusalem can be found in descriptions of architecture in the Bible and Vasari's *Lives*, and the paintings for the four great walls can be located in models from a church, a villa, and a museum all in or near Florence.

The significance of this compendium regarding sources for real art and architecture in the poetry of Robert Browning is that it establishes Browning as a profound student of the objects and history of art and architecture, it provides concrete images for Browning's poetry, and it sets up a basis for the symbolic analysis of his characters and themes. In addition, with the several hundred illustrations (over 70% in color), the extensive Index of Sources with Locations, and the maps of Florence and Rome, this study serves as a collection of and guide to art history. Unspecified and imaginary sources or conflations of sources for art and architecture are also important in matters of history, images, and symbolism, yet they further tell us something about Browning's creative process and the method by which the source hunter should proceed in the future.

In the *Compendium*, under the Summary of Composite Sources, I discuss absentmindedness, poetic license, and factual confusion as possible features of Browning's creative method in using unspecified and especially imaginary conflations of sources for art and architecture. What I now submit is that the factual confusion is indicative of an occasional faulty memory, for a number of times in the *Compendium* I observe that Browning was separated in time and place from points in his travels, that this separation forced him to recall what he had seen, and that this recollection was often dim and therefore prone to error. Error, then, either through absentmindedness or a faulty memory, and/or poetic license—the ambiguous use or deliberate rewriting of history—are what I think led Browning consciously or subconsciously to use composite sources and, for that matter, single unspecified and imaginary sources.

What the source hunter—or literary sleuth, as I prefer to call him—must assume, then, in light of the findings in the *Compendium* and this appendix, is that Browning is ever the serious student of art and architecture conditioned by his absentmindedness, occasional faulty memory, and poetic license; that many times he employs a conflation of sources; and that for these conflations he is drawing on his reading and experience even when he treats his poetry with imaginary mental constructs. Consequently, from these clues into Browning's creative method, the literary sleuth knows that he must do more than search in the library—though that he must do with diligence: he must go into the field, follow Browning's movements, recognize what the poet saw, and make a connection between what he viewed and what he wrote as he did or did not modify what he saw.

Finally, I estimate that in his poetry Robert Browning is the most architectural, sculptural, and, if I may use the term, the most "painterly" of all poets. The *Compendium* and *Appendix A* demonstrate this appraisal by (1) the large number of poems by Browning that use art and architecture; (2) the consistency of Browning's employment of art and architecture in the early, middle, and late periods of his poetic career; (3) the sheer quantity and range of sources entered from the fields of painting, sculpture, and architecture; (4) the diversity of Browning's use of real, unspecified, and imaginary sources for art and architecture, whether those sources are single models or composites; and (5) the wide range of themes and motifs embodied in the symbolism of the art and architecture. I make this claim for Browning's supremacy in the employment of art and architecture with the confidence that, at this time, no comparable compendium on literary art and architecture is on the horizon and with the belief that no other poet, past or present, man or woman, English or otherwise, qualifies for this distinction.

CHRONOLOGY

This chronology lists major events in Browning's life and important readings, travels, and associations with personages contributing to Browning's education and writing about art and architecture. For a general yet more detailed chronology of travels, see Philip Kelley and Ronald Hudson, *The Brownings' Correspondence: a Checklist* (The Browning Institute and Wedgestone Press, 1978), pp. 491-98 (referred to as KELL in this study).

1812   Robert Browning is born on May 7 on Southampton St. in Camberwell, London.

1814   Dulwich Picture Gallery opens and in subsequent years is visited by RB with his father and Alfred Domett.

1826   RB reads Shelley's *Miscellaneous Poems* and *Queen Mab.*

               RB's early education is under the tutelage of his father. He reads the following books containing art and/or about art: Francis Quarles's *Emblems, Divine and Moral*; the Rev. M. Pilkington's *A Dictionary of Painters*; Gerard de Lairesse's *The Art of Painting*; Daniel Bartoli's *Simboli*; George Herbert's *The Temple*; Nathaniel Wanley's *Wonders of the Little World*; the *Biographie universelle*; the books of John Bunyan; the essays of William Hazlitt.

1834   RB visits Aix-la-Chapelle, St. Petersburg.

1836   RB meets D. Maclise.

1838   RB visits Trieste, Venice, Castelfranco, Treviso,

Asolo, Bassano, Solagna, Oliero, Possagno, Verona, Trent, Innsbruck, Munich.

1840   RB and Mrs. Anna Jameson attend Thomas Carlyle's lecture "On Heroes and Hero Worship"; RB meets William Wetmore Story.

1841   RB visits the studio of William Etty in London possibly this early.

1844   RB visits Naples, the Amalfi Coast, Rome; reads extensively in Giorgio Vasari's *Lives*.

1845   RB reads *De la poésie chrétienne*, by Alexis F. Rio.

1846-47   RB marries Elizabeth Barrett on Sept. 12, 1846, in London; travels with her continually until her death in 1861; goes to Paris (meets Mrs. Jameson); travels to Pisa; resides in Casa Guidi, Florence; visits Massa-Carrara, Vallombrosa; meets Hiram Powers in Florence.

1848-49   RB visits Arezzo, Fano, Loreto, Rimini, Bagni di Lucca; reads John Ruskin's *Modern Painters*; Robert Wiedemann Barrett Browning (Pen) is born; RB meets Seymour Kirkup and George Mignaty in Florence.

1850   RB resides briefly near Siena.

1851-52   RB visits Parma, Padua, Venice, Paris (meets Joseph Milsand), London; meets John Ruskin and D. G. Rossetti in London; also meets there, possibly this early, John Millais and Thomas Woolner; returns to Florence; reads in Baldinucci's *Notizie* and familiarizes himself (probably at an earlier date) with guidebooks published by John Murray.

1853   RB makes excursions from Florence to Prato and Bagni di Lucca; visits Assisi; resides in Rome and meets John Gibson, William Page, Lord Leighton, and Harriet Hosmer.

1855-56	RB visits Paris, London.
1858	RB resides at 43 Bocca di Leone, Rome; vacations around Le Havre, France.
1859-60	RB visits Siena, Foligno, Viterbo, Chiusi; visits Castellani's shop in Via Poli, Rome; buys *The Old Yellow Book* in Piazza San Lorenzo, Florence.
1861	EBB dies on June 29 in Casa Guidi and is buried in the Protestant Cemetery, Piazza Donatello, Florence; RB returns to London.
1862	RB vacations in Pornic, France.
1872	RB visits Paris and Fontainebleau.
1877-78	RB visits the Chalet la Saisiaz, near Geneva; stops in Padua on the way from Venice to Paris.
1889	RB visits Asolo; dies in Palazzo Rezzonico, Venice, on Dec. 12; is buried in Westminster Abbey on Dec. 31.

LIST OF ILLUSTRATIONS

CITATIONS AND NOTES

ANDREA DEL SARTO

103-05 (cont. from *Comp.*, 26, 28, 420)

> Yonder's a work now, of that famous youth
> The Urbinate who died five years ago.
> ('T is copied, George Vasari sent it me.)

For an illustration of Raphael's *Pope Leo X with Two Cardinals* and the same subject "copied" by Andrea del Sarto, see Figures 262 and 263 in this appendix. For other allusions to the original version by Raphael, the "Urbinate," see this poem in the *Compendium*, pages 28 and 420, below in this appendix under the next entry, and below under *The Ring and the Book*, Book X, lines 233-35.

259-63 (cont. from *Comp.*, 30, 420)

> In heaven, perhaps, new chances, one more chance—
> Four great walls in the New Jerusalem,
> Meted on each side by the angel's reed,
> For Leonard, Rafael, Agnolo and me
> To cover. . . .

George V. Griffith nominates verses 10-21 from Revelation, chapter 21, as a source for the imaginary "Four great walls in the New Jerusalem, / Meted on each side by the angel's reed" (GRIFF, 371-72). The "angel's reed" is specifically described in verse 15:

> And he that talked with me [one of the seven angels] had a golden reed to measure the city. . . .

With the addition of these verses from Revelation to those sources described in the *Compendium*, pages 30 and 420, all of the elements in Browning's text that combine to encourage forming a composite theory can be explained. The "Four great walls," where paintings by Michelangelo, Leonardo da Vinci, Raphael, and Andrea del Sarto were arranged together at one time—three of the artists in one room, the Tribune—are in the famous Uffizi Gallery, in Florence (Figs. 262, 264-67; Map F:8H). The characterization of the four walls as "great" is based on the extensive proportions of the walls of the Sala Grande of the Villa Medicea, in Poggio a Caiano, where the work of Andrea del Sarto is represented along with that of other artists (Figs. 268, 269). The modifying words "In heaven" are related to the Church of the Santissima Annunziata, in Florence, where Andrea is buried under the chancel and where his work ranges alongside that of other artists in the atrium or Cloister of the Madonna in the church (Figs. 2, 270, 271; Map F:6I,7I). The atrium, Professor Eisenberg informs me, is known in architectural nomenclature as the "paradise" or, to use the more universal term, "*paradisus*," which may tie the fact of Andrea's burial in the Santissima Annunziata with the idea of his being "In heaven" or paradise along with his work in the atrium or *paradisus* of the church (EISE, in conversation, Aug., 1992). And the "New Jerusalem" refers to the celestial city prophesied in Revelation, as entered above in this note; and/or, as recorded in Vasari's *Lives*, it is a reference to Michelozzo's proposed design for a hospital in the terrestrial city of Jerusalem. Michelozzo may be further associated with this hypothesized conflation of varied sources in that he designed the atrium or *paradisus* for the Church of the Santissima Annunziata.

The foregoing discussion, it will be noted, is utilized in the Introduction of this appendix as an example of an imaginary mental construct based on a composite of real elements taken from the fields of architecture and painting, and architecture mentioned in literature—the Bible—and/or a biographical treatise on art—Vasari's *Lives*. For another reference to the "New Jerusalem," described as the "holy Jerusalem" in Revelation (21:10), see below under *Christmas-Eve and Easter-Day* (Pt. I, 10:528-34).

THE BISHOP ORDERS HIS TOMB AT SAINT PRAXED'S CHURCH: ROME, 15—

42, 47-49 (revised and cont. from *Comp.*, **44, 46**)

> Some lump, ah God, of *lapis lazuli,*
> . . .
> So, let the blue lump poise between my knees,
> Like God the Father's globe on both his hands
> Ye worship in the Jesu Church so gay. . . .

Figure 272 displays the monument in the Chapel of St. Ignatius Loyola, and Figure 273 gives in detail the partly visible globe of lapis lazuli, supported by an angel, that surmounts the monument. The globe is the model for the "blue lump" in the text. The Church of the Gesù—"the Jesu Church"—is shown on page 288 of the *Compendium* (Fig. 160), and it appears on the map of Rome (R:8H) just off the Corso Vittorio Emanuele near the Piazza Venezia. The Church of St. Praxed is not on the map of Rome; it is on Via Santa Prassede just south of the Church of Santa Maria Maggiore, which is near the Central Railroad Station.

The Bishop's order, "let the blue lump poise between my knees," is revealing: it egregiously flaunts his sexuality.

BY THE FIRESIDE

14:66-68, 18:86-90 (cont. from *Comp.*, **54-55, 56, 392-93, 423-24**)

> And yonder, at foot of the fronting ridge
>   That takes the turn to a range beyond,
> Is the chapel reached by the one-arched bridge
> . . .
>
> It has some pretension too, this front,
>   With its bit of fresco half-moon-wise
> Set over the porch, Art's early wont:
>   'T is John in the Desert, I surmise,
> But has borne the weather's brunt. . . .

The question arises as to whether or not it matters if the original picture or the facsimile of the Madonna and Child in the Refubbri Chapel was seen by or known to Browning. For several reasons I do not think that Browning's awareness or unawareness of the picture detracts from the nomination of the Madonna and Child as a source or that it is a decisive factor in the formulation of my analysis below and in the *Compendium* (54-55, 56, 423-24). The chapel is fixed in the locale of Browning's poem (CAL; *Comp.*, 392, Fig. 235); the pedimented frame for the picture is built into the wall of the chapel as a permanent fixture (*Comp.*. 393, Fig. 236); and the only image that has been documented as having been in the chapel is that of a Madonna and Child and its facsimile (BAG). The image of a Madonna and Child, then, is permanently related to the Refubbri Chapel and therefore carries a definite involvement in the setting and imagery of the poem. If Browning was not aware of this implication, it is simply a case of the poet writing into the poem, through the word "chapel," more than he knows.

"John in the Desert" is John the Baptist. In the Bible he is the "voice of one crying in the wilderness," the "Desert" in Browning's poem, and he prophesied the coming of Christ (John 1:23-27). Browning, masked as the narrator and John the Baptist through Filippo Lippi's painting of John in the Desert (*Comp.*, 55, 56, Fig. 18), acts as prophet in the poem. He foresees his elective affinity with Elizabeth Barrett and, through his reference to the Refubbri Chapel with its Madonna and Child as a sub-image to the text, adumbrates his marriage to Elizabeth and the birth of their son, Pen. The crescent shape of the "fresco half-moon-wise," presumably "Set over the porch" of the Refubbri Chapel, foreshadows Browning's famous typification of Elizabeth, stated toward the end of "One Word More," as his "moon of poets."

DeVane gives 1853 as the date of composition for "By the Fireside" and 1855 for the genesis of "One Word More" (DEVA, 222, 275). DeVane's association of moon imagery with Elizabeth Barrett Browning (DEVA, 278), as revised here, thus begins two years prior to the writing of "One Word More."

The analysis below under "Parleying with Gerard de Lairesse" (9:230-45, para. two), the reader will note, centers on moon symbolism and the Browning-Ashburton fiasco.

CENCIAJA

15-29 (cont. from *Comp.*, 55, 57, 58)

. . .
. . . Titian['s]. . .

... pictured masterpiece

...

... of the Lady [Beatrice Cenci]. ..

...

... graced our gallery. ....

In this appendix under the Summary of Composite Sources (Cen, 15-29), I enter both the presumed portrait of Beatrice Cenci attributed to Guido Reni, in the Palazzo Corsini, in Rome (*Comp.*, 58, Fig. 19; Map R:8F), and the copy of the same portrait by Hilda, Nathaniel Hawthorne's literary character, as models for Browning's imaginary portrait of a Beatrice Cenci by "Titian."

The following dating, which is not fully specified in the *Compendium* under this poem (*Comp.*, 55, 57), clarifies the biographical evidence in support of Hilda's copy of Beatrice Cenci, from Chapter VII, "Beatrice," in Hawthorne's *The Marble Faun*, as one of the composite sources. The Hawthornes visited the Brownings in Casa Guidi in 1858 (*Comp.*, 57); *The Marble Faun* was published in 1860; Browning's copy of *The Marble Faun*, which was in his library under the alternate title of *Transformation: or, the Romance of Monte Beni*, has "Rome 1869" written on the title page (KEL, 99, item A1155); and "Cenciaja" is given the date 1876 on Browning's manuscript of the poem (DEVA, 410).

Hawthorne, in *The Marble Faun*, uses the presumed portrait of Beatrice Cenci in the Palazzo Corsini and the copy by Hilda as portents recalling the murder of Beatrice's father and foreseeing the murder of Miriam's husband. Browning, in "Cenciaja," imputes the portrait of Beatrice Cenci to Titian, rather than Guido Reni, in order to imply the sensuality on the part of Beatrice's father that led to his being murdered for sexually abusing Beatrice.

Browning also employs Titian's art as a symbol of sensuality in other poems, namely in "Any Wife to Any Husband" (*Comp.*, 30-31, Fig. 5), "In a Gondola" (*Comp.*, 143, 146, 147, Fig. 73), and "Porphyria's Lover" (see this poem below, lines 38-41). The nude paintings by Titian of Venus and Mary Magdalen, which are implied in these poems, are clearly sensual.

CHRISTMAS-EVE AND EASTER-DAY (half-titles used in *Comp.*)

Pt.I,10:528-34 (cont. from *Comp.*, 62-63, revised numbering)

> Is it really on the earth,
> This miraculous Dome of God?
> Has the angel's measuring-rod
> Which numbered cubits, gem from gem,
> 'Twixt the gates of the New Jerusalem,
> Meted it out,—and what he meted,
> Have the sons of men completed?

The "New Jerusalem" or "holy Jerusalem" is described in Revelation, chapter 21, verses 10-21 (PET, I, 1104; KING, V, 343; JACK, IV, 350). The "angel's measuring-rod," in verse 15, is a "golden reed" used by one of the seven angels to "measure the city." Compare with the citation above under "Andrea del Sarto," lines 259-63, for a similar reference to the "New Jerusalem."

For the detailed delineation of the Church of Saint Peter in the Vatican—the "miraculous Dome of God"—that follows this citation, see the *Compendium* (62-63, 248-49, Figs. 133, 134). Boyd Litzinger assesses Browning's description of Vatican display as "sensual" in appeal (LIT, 22-23); my treatment in the next entry, based on sculptural sources both real and literary, modifies Litzinger's thesis of anti-Catholicism in Browning's poem.

Pt.I,12:749-52, 764-68 (cont. from *Comp.*, 63-64, revised numbering)

> . . .
> But, now and then, [the artist] bravely aspires to consummate
> A Colossus by no means so easy to come at,
> And uses the whole of his block for the bust,
> Leaving the mind of the public to finish it,
> . . .
> Some artist of another ambition,
> Who having a block to carve, no bigger,
> Has spent his power on the opposite quest,
> And believed to begin at the feet was best—
> For so may I see, ere I die, the whole figure!

In the context of these passages, Browning describes how an artist with a large "block" of marble for fashioning a "Colossus" will use the block to make only the "bust" of the colossus, since the block is not large enough for the whole statue. Then Browning reverses the procedure and considers using the block for one of the "feet." In both cases, whether the sculptor begins with the head or feet, the viewer will have to use his imagination to complete the "whole figure."

As possible sources for Browning's colossus, two huge fragmented stone statues come to mind. One is literary: the statue of Ozymandias from Shelley's poem of the same name; the other is real: the enormous head and both feet of Constantine the Great, in the courtyard of the Conservatori Museum, in Rome (Map R:8H, 8I). The image in which the artist in Browning's poem decides "to begin at the feet" owes something to lines 2 and 3 in Shelley's poem, "Two vast and trunkless legs of stone / Stand in the desert"; the bust in Browning's text corresponds with the image in lines 3 and 4 of Shelley's poem, "Near them [that is, near the legs], on the sand, / Half sunk, a shattered visage lies." The gigantic head of Constantine the Great has already been put forth as a source for the poem "Protus" (*Comp.*, 251, 252, Fig. 136). Figure 300 exhibits one of the huge feet from the statue.

A third consideration is the famous *Colossus of Rhodes*. Commentators, including myself, have consistently advanced the defunct statue, once in the harbor of Rhodes, as a source (KRY, 140; KING, V, 344; PET, I, 1104; JACK, IV, 358; *Comp.*, 63-64). But the *Colossus of Rhodes* was made of bronze, and bronze is not an appropriate material for Browning's "block to carve." Accordingly, I retract the *Colossus of Rhodes* as a viable model and do not enter it below in the Summary of Composite Sources under the citation given here.

For Shelley, the remaining legs of his colossus stand for oblivion, the fate of all tyrants like Ozymandias. But, as a model for Browning's text above, the isolated legs of Shelley's colossus represent a criticism of Roman Catholicism. Following the sensuous, even sensual description of the Church of St. Peter in the Vatican, which occurs in sections 10 and 11 (*Comp.*, 62-63, 248-249, Figs. 133, 134; see the preceding entry), Browning, in section 12, intimates that Roman Catholicism is ritualistic (DEVA, 197), that the lower parts of his own and Shelley's colossus symbolize a physical religion on foot and knee, so to speak, a pedestrian religion of pilgrimages and genuflections for the common, undiscriminating man rather than the more intellectually oriented. In the opening lines of section 12 Browning states his position fully:

> So I summed up my new resolves:
> Too much love there can never be.
> And where the intellect devolves
> Its function on love exclusively,

> I, a man who possesses both,
> Will accept the provision, nothing loth,
> —Will feast my love, then depart elsewhere,
> That my intellect may find its share.

The literary colossus of Ozymandias, without a trunk, is bottom-heavy with legs; as a model for the lower part of Browning's colossus, they stand for a physical approach to religion that Browning calls "love." The head or "visage" of Ozymandias, symbolizing the "intellect" or mind, is "shattered." The huge head and feet of Constantine the Great, however, are intact. They suggest a corrective balance to the image of disproportion in Shelley's poem, for Constantine the Great, as the first Roman Catholic emperor, was a man of considerable faith *and* intelligence.

Moreover, Browning's use of Cardinal Newman as one of the models for the Bishop in his subsequent poem "Bishop Blougram's Apology" (THOM, 27-28) points up Browning's awareness, no doubt at the time he wrote *Christmas-Eve and Easter-Day*, of another outstanding Roman Catholic whose religious view was devotional yet rational.

More about the enormous bust of Constantine the Great is entered below under "Protus," lines 52-57.

CLEON

82, 88-94 (cont. from *Comp.*, 65, 66-67)

> See, in the chequered pavement opposite,
> . . .
> Making at last a picture; there it lies.
> So, first the perfect separate forms were made,
> The portions of mankind; and after, so,
> Occurred the combination of the same.
> For where had been a progress, otherwise?
> Mankind, made up of all the single men,—
> In such a synthesis the labor [sic] ends.

The pavement in the Duomo of Siena, which is proposed as a source in the *Compendium* (65, 66-67, Figs. 22 and 23), is made up of forty-three polychromic marble panels by over forty sixteenth-century artists, including, most notably, Beccafumi (SIE, 70-74). These panels, as I see them, represent the "labor" of "all the single men," the individual artists, the "portions of mankind" in Browning's text. The subjects of the panels are secular, mythological, and Christian, with Allegories, Sibyls, and Virtues being placed with scenes from the Old Testament in "synthesis," that is, in the form of a Latin cross. The lower part or foot of the cross depicts the secular and mythological scenes, while the transecting and upper parts of the cross are exclusively Christian. Two of the mythological figures are, appropriately enough, the Cumean Sibyl and the Erythrean Sibyl, who foretold the coming of Christ (cf. BER, 215; cf. the legend of the Sibyl that appeared to Augustus, *Comp.*, 140, 141-142, Figs. 69, 70). This arrangement of Christian scenes by various artists positioned over the secular and pagan ones in the cross coordinates with that part of Browning's text which states, "For where had been a progress, otherwise?"

Progress here signifies the familiar doctrine-of-the-imperfect theme and Browning's preference for Christian art to pagan art. Greco-Roman or pagan art is technically perfect, idealistic in conception, and, for the most part, anonymous in authorship. Christian art is imperfectly conceived, yet it is more realistic and expressive of individualistic style (DEVA, 251; EISE). Browning develops the importance of artistic individualism in "Old Pictures in Florence" (see below under Old, 26:201-02) and promulgates his preference for realism in "Parleying with Gerard de Lairesse" (see below under Parl, 5:116-26, para. 5).

On the other hand, in view of Christianity as religion and not art history, Adrienne Munich advances George Herbert's "The Church Floor" as a source for the text at hand (MU, 130-32). Several reasons support this hypothesis: Browning was familiar with Herbert's writings (KEL, 100, item A1171); the word "checker'd," which appears in line 5 of Herbert's poem, is in correspondence with Browning's "checkered pavement"; and the Christian theme of Herbert's poem is appropriate to that of Browning's verses.

Given this additional source, I venture that the pavement in the Duomo of Siena and Herbert's "The Church Floor" were conflated in Browning's mind. This notion follows from the use of emblems for synthesis in the two sources and the five-fold complementary Christian symbolism of the floorings involved. "The Church Floor," as we know, is a single poem in Herbert's large literary work, *The Temple*. Emblematically, the image of Herbert's temple as a body of writings embracing a number of single poems forms a literary whole, and the flooring of his temple, as a church, makes up part of an architectural whole; in a similar manner, the image of a Latin cross shapes into an overall design all the single pictures on the pavement of the Duomo of Siena. Symbolically, Herbert's church floor entails five Christian Virtues: Patience, Humility, Confidence, Love, and Charity; the upper part of the Latin cross forming the pavement of the Duomo of Siena depicts five other Christian Virtues: Prudence, Temperance, Mercy, Justice, and Fortitude (SIE, 71-72).

As models for the imaginary checkered pavement of Cleon's courtyard, the church floor of Herbert's poem and the pavement of the Duomo of Siena act as composite images of a subtext in opposition to Cleon's rejection of Christianity.

174-76 (revised from *Comp.*, 65, 424-25)

> . . . what survives myself?
> The brazen statue [of Protus] to o'erlook my grave,
> Set on the promontory which I named.

There is no statue for the imaginary Cleon, as misread into the *Compendium* (65, 424-25). It is the imaginary King Protus who speaks of the "brazen statue to o'erlook my grave." But this error in name does not materially affect the argument for the statue of the Grand Duke Ferdinand I, by Giovanni da Bologna, in Arezzo (*Comp.*, 305, Fig. 172), as a model for the statue of Browning's imaginary King Protus.

THE ENGLISHMAN IN ITALY: PIANO DI SORRENTO

207-18 (cont. from *Comp.*, 79-81)

> . . . there slumbered
>   As greenly as ever
> Those isles of the siren, your Galli;
>   No ages can sever
> The Three, nor enable their sister
>   To join them,—halfway
> On the voyage, she looked at Ulysses—
>   No farther to-day,
> Though the small one, just launched in the wave
>   Watches breast-high and steady
> From under the rock, her bold sister
>   Swum halfway already.

Rowena Fowler establishes a strong biographical relationship between the siren motif during the courtship of the Brownings and William Etty's painting *The Sirens and Ulysses*. The picture was exhibited in 1837 and is now housed in the Manchester City Art Gallery. Browning visited Etty's studio in Buckingham Street, presented Etty with a copy of *Dramatic Lyrics*, and wrote to him before Etty's death in 1849: "We have often remembered your grand *Sirens*" (FOW, 32-33, 46, n. 7; HOO, 26).

Fowler, however, does not relate Etty's picture to "The Englishman in Italy" either in general or particular; this I shall proceed to do in detail.

Looking at Figure 274, we see that there are correspondences in number and gender between Etty's painting and Browning's text. The three nude figures in Etty's picture represent, in Browning's poem, the three main islands among the five islands of the Galli group, "Those isles of the siren, your Galli. . . The Three," which are about three and a half miles southwest of the Italian town of Positano. The words "sister," "she," and "her" indicate that Browning personifies the five islands as women; specifically, the "sister," "she," or "her" is the fourth island, the one that is about one mile and a half west of the main group of three islands and thus cannot "join" the other three. The fifth island, the "small one" off shore "just launched in the wave," about a mile or so northwest of the fourth island, "Watches breast-high. . . her bold sister [the fourth island] / Swum halfway already." Browning's poem further coordinates with Etty's picture by suggesting why there are only three sirens in the painting. The fourth island as a siren "looked at Ulysses" but did not sing to him; she had "Swum halfway" but had not joined the three islands or sirens grouped together when the boat of Ulysses and his men passed by them. The fifth island or siren was too far away to be involved and only watched the fourth island, "her bold sister," swimming. (More about the Galli Islands and the myth of Ulysses is described in WOO, II, 352-53, note for lines 200-08.)

Etty's painting is symbolic of the elopement of the Brownings to Italy, which is in keeping with my discussion in the *Compendium* (79-81, Fig. 32) of King Robert's Tower, on the largest of the Galli Islands, as an emblem of a recurring motif in the correspondence of the Brownings, their siren song (KIN, I, 273).

EURYDICE TO ORPHEUS: A PICTURE BY LEIGHTON

1-8 (cont. from *Comp.*, 86-89)

> But give them me, the mouth, the eyes, the brow!
> Let them once more absorb me! One look now
>   Will lap me round forever, not to pass
> Out of its light, though darkness lie beyond:
> Hold me but safe again within the bond
>   Of one immortal look! All woe that was,
> Forgotten, and all terror that may be,
> Defied,—no past is mine, no future: look at me!

If it is conceded, as I argue in the *Compendium*, that the tomb of Elizabeth Barrett Browning and the story of Orpheus and Eurydice establish Florence as the setting for Browning's poem (*Comp.*, 88-89), then Shelley's "Ode to the West Wind," as I contend here, strengthens the connection. At the end of the "Ode," Shelley personifies himself implicitly as the lyre of Orpheus in the form of forested trees as strings of the lyre played upon by the West Wind: "Make me thy lyre, even as the forest is" (line 57). Earlier in the poem the antecedent for the personification of Shelley as Orpheus is implied in the reference to "some fierce Maenad" (line 21), who represents the Maenads of mythology who tore Orpheus to pieces. And in the prefatory note to the "Ode," Shelley designates the West Wind as that in the "wood that skirts the Arno," the river of course that runs through Florence. Florence, then, as represented by Elizabeth's tomb and the West Wind of Shelley's poem, acts as a locale for the Orpheus motif in Browning's poem.

Of further relevance to the personification of Shelley as a lyre in his "Ode" are the three lyres carved on the tomb of Elizabeth Barrett Browning. The lyres were designed by Frederic Leighton, and he explains their significance in a rather unpunctuated letter that is quoted by Ormond (ORMO, 76):

> the three styles of poetry in which she [Elizabeth Barrett Browning] shone—typified by three harps—the celestial harp . . . the classic lyre harp with trag. & com. masks and laurel and the more modern Italian lute with the star of Italy the broken chains and the wreath of flowers—the joy at the liberation of Italy. Mrs. B's day dream. The idea of having 3 harps was Browning's[;] the detailed working out of his thoughts is mine.

Figure 37 (*Comp.*, 88) features the medallion on Elizabeth's tomb that displays the "modern Italian lute with the star of Italy the broken chains and the wreath of flowers—the joy of the liberation of Italy. Mrs. B's daydream." From this medallion it is a short leap to the archetypal criticism of Shelley's "Ode" as a protest against the Congress of Vienna in 1815 (BLO, 447)—and the resulting territorial gains by Austria from Italy—to an adumbration of independence by Italy in 1870. Shelley's concluding "trumpet" of a "prophecy," through which blows the West Wind of Florence, announces the "Winter" of the Austrian occupation of Italy to be followed by the "Spring" of the Risorgimento.

Furthermore, a deep-rooted interpretation applies to not just one but to all of the lyres on the tomb of Elizabeth Barrett Browning. Robert Browning, as noted above in Leighton's letter, is credited with the general conception of the lyres on Elizabeth's tomb, and he, in addition to his wife, cannot be disassociated from their symbolism. As images of a subtext to the poem, the lyres represent not only Elizabeth's Italian lute of nationalism—as we have seen—but also the instrument for the music of Orpheus and the music or prosody of Robert's verses. One can even imagine the lyres on Elizabeth's tomb being played upon by the West Wind over the Arno River, just as Shelley's forested trees of poetry in the Arno Woods, acting as the lyre of the West Wind, are played upon by the West Wind.

The lyrics of Orpheus relate to the persona of Elizabeth as Eurydice, and the verses of Robert, as Orpheus, memorializing Elizabeth as Eurydice, perpetuate Elizabeth's memory in Florence. That Browning was aware of an image of himself as Orpheus is evident from an early letter of 1846 in which Elizabeth, writing to Browning, refers to him as "my Orpheus" (KIN, I, 532). Browning, as I point out in the *Compendium* (89), did not return to Florence after Elizabeth's tomb was completed. He thus, in a figurative sense, avoided the tragedy that befell Orpheus and Eurydice: by not looking back on Elizabeth, that is, on her tomb, Browning averted having what the text calls "no future," and he retained his hope for an afterlife with Elizabeth.

Other decorative motifs either on or related to the tomb of Elizabeth Barrett Browning are developed below under "Flute-Music, with an Accompaniment" (46-48), "Parleying with Gerard de Lairesse" (16:426-34), and *The Ring and the Book* (I.1-4, 15-17).

FIFINE AT THE FAIR

4:28

> 'T was not for every Gawain to gaze upon the Grail!

This passage corroborates my nomination of Tennyson's *Idylls of the King* with illustrations by Gustave Doré (1869) as a source for "Doré's last picture-book," which is described in the last line of section 35 in *Fifine at the Fair* (*Comp.*, 91-92). In the chapter titled "The Holy Grail" of Tennyson's poem, the text in verse paragraph 52 reads:

> 'Nay, lord,' said Gawain, 'not for such as I.
> Therefore I communed with a saintly man,
> Who made me sure the quest was not for me. . . .'

By implication, spiritual quest was neither for Sir Gawain nor Browning's worldly Don Juan (RYAL, 48-49, SOU, 51-52).

Section 47

> . . .
> With Gérôme well at work,—observe how brow recedes,
> Head shudders back on spine, as if one haled the hair,
> Would have the full-face front what pin-point eye's
>   sharp stare
> Announces; mouth agape to drink the flowing fate,
> While chin protrudes to meet the burst o' the wave. . .
> . . .
> And who wants Horror, has it.

I doubt that this section describes a painting by "Gérôme," especially in light of Barbara Melchiori's unsuccessful effort to find a corresponding picture by that artist (MELC, 174). More likely, the section is one of several descriptions by Browning of the pictures of Andromeda by both Polidoro da Caravaggio and Volpato, for the text has elements that correspond with both pictures either together or separately. Specifically, the portraits of Andromeda (*Comp.*, 225, 226, Figs. 121, 122) show her face in profile so that clearly the "brow recedes" and the "Head shudders back on spine, as if [some other] one haled the hair," and so that her "pin-point eyes sharp stare / Announces" the waving hair seen from her "full-face front." Only the version by Volpato, however, (Fig. 122) depicts the force confronting the "chin [that] protrudes [sideways] to meet the burst o' the wave," for the action of the wave in the Polidoro da Caravaggio can hardly be called a "burst." Neither version has a "mouth agape," but the mouth in the Polidoro da Caravaggio is more open than that in the Volpato.

Other discussions also point out the differences between the renditions of Andromeda by Polidoro da Caravaggio and Volpato; they are laid out below under this poem (section 49), under *Pauline* (656-67), and *The Ring and the Book* (VI.1987-96, VII.390-93, and IX.965-70).

Section 48

> Who wants some other show
> Of soul, may seek elsewhere—this second [drawing]
> 　　　of the row?
> What does it give for germ, monadic mere intent
> Of mind in face, faint first of meanings ever meant?
> Why, possibly, a grin, that, strengthened, grows a laugh;
> That, softened, leaves a smile; that, tempered, bids
> 　　　you quaff
> At such a magic cup as English Reynolds once
> Compounded: for the witch pulls out of you response
> Like Garrick's to Thalia, however due may be
> Your homage claimed by that stiff-stoled Melpomene!

The picture that "English [Sir Joshua] Reynolds once / Compounded" is unquestionably the portrait of David Garrick caught between "Thalia" and "Melpomene," the goddesses of comedy and tragedy, respectively (SOU, 90-91; PET, II, 979; Fig. 275). The David Garrick of theatrical fame in the eighteenth century was indeed known equally for his portrayals of comedy and tragedy, and Browning plays particularly on the depiction by Reynolds of Thalia, Comedy, by giving her an expression that is "possibly, a grin, that, strengthened, grows a laugh; / That, softened, leaves a smile." At the same time, "stiff-stoled Melpomene" reveals her displeasure with Garrick for not heeding her exhortation to play tragedy. Horace Walpole sums up the picture as follows (HIL, opposite p. 92):

> Garrick between Tragedy and Comedy. The former exhorts him to follow her exalted vocation, but Comedy drags him away, and he seems to yield willingly, though endeavouring to excuse himself, and pleading that he is forced.

No doubt David Garrick represents Don Juan in this portrait, Thalia stands for Fifine, and Melpomene embodies Elvire (SOU, 90-91). Thalia or Comedy as Fifine expresses Don Juan's lighthearted attachment to the gypsy, and Melpomene or Tragedy as Elvire emphasizes Don Juan's serious relationship with his wife.

Section 49

> And just this one face more! Pardon the bold pretence!
> May there not lurk some hint, struggle toward evidence
> In that compressed mouth, those strained nostrils,
>   steadfast eyes
> Of utter passion, absolute self-sacrifice,
> Which—could I but subdue the wild grotesque, refine
> That bulge of brow, make blunt that nose's aquiline,
> And let, although compressed, a point of pulp appear
> I' the mouth—would give at last the portrait of Elvire?

Browning, I believe, as in section 47, is drawing on the versions of Andromeda painted by Polidoro da Caravaggio and etched by Volpato. The profile of the face is again rendered, but this time the focus is on the "bulge of brow," the "nose's aquiline," and the "compressed mouth." The bulge of the brow is common to both paintings but is most prominent in the Polidoro da Caravaggio; whereas the compressed mouth is most noticeable in the Volpato. Touches of the aquiline can be traced in both faces, but I think that the Polidoro da Caravaggio has more of the aspect of a bird's—if not an eagle's—beak (*Comp.*, 225, 226, Figs. 121, 122).

If we assume that this "portrait of Elvire" is connected with Andromeda, then sections 47, 48, and 49 coordinate in a triptych "draw[n]" by Don Juan with a "piece of broken pipe" on the "sand" (section 45). The two pictures of Andromeda, the Polidoro da Caravaggio and the Volpato, are positioned as the wings of the triptych; the picture by Reynolds (Fig. 275) lies between the wings. Elvire as Andromeda expresses "absolute self-sacrifice" in section 49 and the "Horror" involved in that sacrifice in section 47. The tug of war in section 48, placed between sections 47 and 49, pits Elvire as Melpomene against Fifine as Thalia; Melpomene and Thalia are vying for the affection of David Garrick, who represents Don Juan. The portraits of Andromeda as Elvire, as frames to the central action in the triptych, serve dramatically to heighten but not resolve the conflict among Elvire, Fifine, and Don Juan.

123:2109-12

> . . . at bottom of the rungs
> O' the ladder, Jacob saw, where heavenly angels stept
> Up and down, lay a stone which served him, while
>   he slept,
> For pillow. . . .

Aert de Gelder's painting *Jacob's Dream* is proposed as a source in *The Ring and the Book* (*Comp.*, 281, 282, Fig. 157), and I think that it also provides a model for this passage. The identifying feature in the text is the hard bedding upon which Jacob sleeps while experiencing his dream: as can be seen in the lower left-hand corner of the painting, there "lay a stone which served him, while he slept, / For pillow."

Also, see below under *The Ring and the Book*, Book I, lines 1391-94, 1397-98.

FLUTE-MUSIC, WITH AN ACCOMPANIMENT

46-48

> Daisied turf gives room to
> Trefoil, plucked once in her presence—
> Growing by her tomb too!

Natural and ornamental images of flowers indicate that this citation is an allusion to the grave of Elizabeth Barrett Browning, to "her tomb" in the Protestant Cemetery of Piazza Donatello, in Florence. The "Dais[y]" as a natural and sculptural emblem relates to the tomb of and stands for Mrs. Browning; it receives treatment below under the earlier poem "Parleying with Gerard de Lairesse," section 16, lines 426-34. The "Trefoil" as a clover and as an architectural Gothic arch also represents Mrs. Browning and relates to her tomb; central to the development of this idea are several facts. Five Gothic trefoil arches are built into the side wall of the Church of San Felice, in Florence. In *The Ring and the Book*, Book I, lines 479-82, Browning describes this side wall, which is "opposite" the "narrow terrace" of Casa Guidi, as "Felice-church-side stretched" (*Comp.*, 269, 272, 342, Fig. 197; Map F:9G). And the Italian name "Felice" means "happy" in English. Taken together, these facts suggest Elizabeth's happy life in Casa Guidi—her life of felicity next to the Church of San Felice—to the time of her death and burial in Piazza Donatello, and they link her with the trefoils as clovers growing around her tomb and the trefoils as Gothic arches facing Casa Guidi.

A related citation combining lines 1, 2, 11, and 12 from stanza 1 alludes to the Browning-Ashburton debacle:

> *He.* AH [sic], the bird-like fluting
>   Through the ash-tops yonder—
>   . . .
> Love, no doubt, nay, love excessive
>   'T is, your ash-tops curtain.

Strikingly, the name of Louisa, Lady Ashburton, is suggested by the words "ash-tops curtain"; yet, to my knowledge, this implied rhyme—"ash. . . curtain"/Ashburton—has been noted in Browning studies by no other commentator. Browning's "love excessive" for Elizabeth, represented by the music of the "bird-like fluting," is temporarily "curtain[ed]" by Lady Ashburton, by the tops of the ash trees. Similarly, in "Parleying with Daniel Bartoli" (17:285-86), written only three years previously, the moon, as Elizabeth, is obscured by a cloud, as Lady Ashburton (DEVA, 503-04; also see below under Parl, 9:230-45, para. 2). In all, Browning employs the compound word "ash-tops" seven times in "Flute-Music, with an Accompaniment" (lines 2, 12, 13, 131, 137, 170, and 181): it is as if, in keeping with the musical nature of the poem, "ash-tops curtain" is a theme with six variations on Lady Ashburton as "obstruction" (line 38)—obstruction, that is, of the memory of Elizabeth Barrett Browning. As Figure 37 shows (*Comp.*, 88), trees are near the tomb of Elizabeth Barrett Browning; I have not determined if any of them are ash trees.

A FORGIVENESS

271-77

> And mark the handle's dim pellucid green,
> Carved, the hard jadestone, as you pinch a bean,
> Into a sort of parrot-bird! He pecks
> A grape-bunch; his two eyes are ruby-specks
> Pure from the mine: seen this way,—glassy blank,
> But turn them,—lo, the inmost fire, that shrank
> From sparkling, sends a red dart right to aim!

The entry in *The Browning Collections* for this dagger owned by

Browning is as follows (KEL, 506, item H439):

> Sind Peshkabz and Scabbard. Green jade hilt carved as a bird
> pecking at fruit; scabbard has gilt copper mounts; bequeathed to
> RB by Ernest Benzon; described in RB's 1876 poem "A Forgive-
> ness." *Browning Collections*, lot 1297, purchased by Maggs.

The dagger serves as a model for the husband's instrument of vengeance in Browning's poem; the color imagery of
the red and green jewels on the hilt of the dagger symbolizes the
vengeance with an underlying tone of jealousy. The point of the
blade, which is used to write the wife's confession in her own
blood (lines 369-75), is like the "red dart" that glints from the
"ruby-specks" of the "two eyes" of the "parrot-bird" on the hilt.
And the "handle's dim pellucid green" from the "jadestone"
calls to mind the familiar "green-ey'd monster" of "jealousy" associated with Shakespeare's Moor of Venice (*Othello*, III.iii.165-
66). Coordinate with the green eyes of jealousy in Shakespeare's
play are the red eyes of vengeance in Browning's poem.

A GRAMMARIAN'S FUNERAL: SHORTLY AFTER THE REVIVAL OF LEARNING IN EUROPE

13-16 (cont. from *Comp.*, 430)

> Leave we the unlettered plain its herd and crop;
>   Seek we sepulture
> On a tall mountain, citied to the top,
>   Crowded with culture!

In a literal sense, San Marino, as a locale for Browning's poem, is
"Crowded with culture." Aside from a thriving crafts industry,
it boasts a number of architectural features and several museums. Architectural highlights, in addition to the three towers
described in the *Compendium* (p. 391, Fig. 234, p. 430), are the
Palazzo Governo and the Basilica of San Marino. The museums, which are rich and varied, comprise two picture galleries, a
coin and stamp museum, and an arms museum. The picture
galleries display paintings ranging from the twelfth through the
seventeenth centuries and include Egyptian, Etruscan, and Roman items, especially pottery, coins, statuettes, and funerary objects.

The phrase "Seek we sepulture" indicates, no doubt, a

prideful desire by the disciples to erect for their master, the grammarian, a monumental tomb. David DeLaura suggests that a source for this pride of burial could be John Ruskin's chapter "Roman Renaissance," sections 46-84, in *Stones of Venice, III* (RUS, XI, 81-114). There, Ruskin treats Venetian "Pride of State" through "sepulchral monuments," "sepulchral architecture," and "statues" (DELAU, 116, n. 44).

31-34

> He, whom we convoy to his grave aloft,
>   Singing together,
> He was a man born with thy face and throat,
>   Lyric Apollo!

I propose that the home of the Greek gods of mythology, Olympus, is part of a composite architectural setting for this poem. The idea of Olympus as a locale derives from the characterization of the grammarian as "Apollo" in Browning's text and from the possible influence of the description of Apollo in Matthew Arnold's earlier poem "Empedocles on Etna," which was published in 1852. My nomination of the citadels of San Marino as a setting (*Comp.*, p. 391, Fig. 234, p. 430; see the preceding entry) conflates with the conception of Olympus as a source in conjunction with the passage below from Arnold's poem.

At the conclusion of "Empedocles on Etna," Apollo and the Nine Muses are depicted by Callicles en route to Olympus (lines 445-46, 452, 455-56):

> 'T is Apollo comes leading
> His choir, the Nine.
> . . .
> The glorified train. . .
> . . .
> Then on to Olympus,
> Their endless abode.

The disciples of Browning's grammarian, "Singing together" as they carry the grammarian, "Lyric Apollo," in "convoy" up to the citadel, resemble Arnold's "Apollo" and "His choir, the Nine" on their way in "train" up to "Olympus, / Their endless abode." The top of the citadel in Browning's poem is "Crowded with culture" (see preceding entry); in Arnold's poem Apollo and the Nine Muses, as representatives of the arts in Olympus, are, so to speak, a crowd of culture in and of themselves.

The possible influence of Arnold on Browning, which helps in establishing Olympus as a setting for Browning's poem, is brought out by David DeLaura in Appendix I to his essay "Ruskin, Arnold, and Browning's Grammarian." DeLaura explains in Appendix I, titled Browning and Arnold's "Empedocles on Etna," that Browning recommended to Arnold that Arnold reprint the "Empedocles" poem because, aside from his opinion of its content, Browning admired the poem. DeLaura goes on to point out the Callicles sections as ideal models for Browning to have emulated in developing a more "detached" style (DELAU, 103). It is the Callicles section at the end of the poem, I remind the reader, that contains the reference to Apollo given here; thus DeLaura's theory is confirmed, since the characterization in Browning's poem of the grammarian as Apollo is a literary example of detachment.

As interpretation, the use of a figure from Greek mythology to personify Browning's grammarian operates in various symbolic ways. The grammarian, as "Lyric Apollo," is a Greek scholar not only with a specialty in grammar but also with an interest in prosody, prosody being what I think the word "Lyric" implies. The grammarian is an expert in grammar because "He settled *Hoti's* business. . . Properly based *Oun*—/ Gave us the doctrine of the enclitic *De*" (lines 129-31); he is a student of prosody because he planned to pursue "New measures, other feet anon" (line 39). Then, too, the grammarian, as Apollo, is the God of Light, who admits to no darkness; he is the God of Truth who demands, "Let me know all!" (line 61). Finally, since the mythic Olympus is the habitation of the Greek gods and is associated with the real Mount Olympus in Thessaly, the highest mountain in Greece, the grammarian, seeking truth as Apollo ascending Olympus, represents soaring aspiration in Browning's Doctrine of the Imperfect (lines 113-20):

> That low man seeks a little thing to do,
>   Sees it and does it:
> This high man, with a great thing to pursue,
>   Dies ere he knows it.
> That low man goes on adding one to one,
>   His hundred's soon hit:
> This high man, aiming at a million,
>   Misses an unit.

Compare with the image of the "British Grenadiers" that Browning uses later in "Parleying with Charles Avison" at the end of section 9: they are "Titanic striding toward Olympus!"

IN A BALCONY

515-20

> [Queen.]
> Who cares to see the fountain's very shape,
> Whether it be a Triton's or a Nymph's
> That pours the foam, makes rainbows all around?
> You could not praise indeed the empty conch;
> But I'll pour floods of love and hide myself.
> How I will love him!

In a Balcony was probably written between July, 1853, and June, 1854 (DEVA, 252), during which time the Brownings visited Rome and no doubt saw Bernini's famous *Triton Fountain*, in Piazza Barberini. Years later, while writing *The Ring and the Book*, Browning was to describe the fountain explicitly and fully (*Comp.*, 274, 277, 278-79, Figs. 154, 155; Map R:7I).

The water that flows from the "fountain," like that from the "conch" of the *Triton Fountain* stands for the passion that the Queen has for Norbert: she will "pour floods of love" on him.

INAPPREHENSIVENESS

3-4, 12-14

> How it towers
> Yonder, the ruin o'er this vale of ours!
> . . .
> . . .   noticed here at Asolo
> That certain weed-growths on the ravaged wall
> Seem [to be]. . . .

This poem was written while Browning was a guest of Mrs. Bronson in Asolo; at the same time he wrote to Mrs. Thomas FitzGerald the following letter dated October 8, 1889 (ORR, 389):

> I find the turret [in Asolo] rather the worse for careful weeding—the hawks which used to build there have been "shot for food"—and the echo is sadly curtailed of its replies. . . .

William DeVane, Betty Miller, and Michael Meredith identify the turret that "towers" in "Asolo" as Queen Catherine Cornaro's Castle, which is part of the locale in *Pippa Passes*, Part II, lines 271-74 (MIL, 277-78; DEVA, 533; MERE, lviii; *Comp.*, pp. 234, 235, Figs. 126, 127, p. 241). John Pettigrew and Thomas Collins, however, believe that the "ruin" is La Rocca or the old Castle of Asolo, the setting for Part III in *Pippa Passes* (PET, II, 1123; *Comp.*, 234, Fig. 126).

DeVane, Miller, Meredith, and Pettigrew and Collins concur that the poem is based on a real experience, and except for Pettigrew and Collins, who do not comment, they interpret the title of the poem as the missed moment of rapport when the woman, Mrs. Bronson, is "inapprehensive" (line 25) to the "dormant passion" (lines 23, 29) of the man, Robert Browning (DEVA, 533-34; MIL, 277-78; MERE, lviii-lx; PET, II, 1123).

I maintain that the landmarks in question are composite sources and that emblematically they bolster the above biographical interpretation. With the focus on the "missing turret" in line 9 of Browning's poem, we know architecturally that La Rocca is being described (see the photograph of La Rocca in MERE, opposite page lii, which displays a surviving turret and two missing turrets). But geographically, if we assume that Browning is viewing the sunset, the "West's faint flare" (lines 5, 26), from the loggia of La Mura, which was his wont while staying with Mrs. Bronson (MIL, 277; MERE, 132-33), only Queen Cornaro's Castle, not La Rocca, is visible to the west of the loggia.

The Castle of Queen Catherine Cornaro associates with Mrs. Bronson emblematically because she, *Katherine* Bronson, used the Queen's name, *Catherine* Cornaro (italics mine), as a nom-de-plume in 1882 for an article on Burano lace (MERE, lxxiv, n. 17). The "West's faint flare" of the sunset as it frames Catherine Cornaro's Castle, as viewed from Katherine Bronson's home, forms an emblem for Mrs. Bronson's dim response to the fire of Browning's "dormant passion." La Rocca symbolizes the missed moment of rapport between Browning and Mrs. Bronson because in 1889 Browning could not demonstrate to her the "echo," then "sadly curtailed of its replies," that he had heard there in 1838 and 1878 (MERE, 102, n. 3, 140). And the depiction of La Rocca as a "ruin" with a "missing turret" and a "ravaged wall" heightens the symbolism with the implied effect that something is amiss in the relationship.

That something amiss is especially sexual if the turret is

considered a phallic symbol. The words "ravaged" and "ruin" also seem to have sexual connotations, though how they might apply to Mrs. Bronson and Browning biographical evidence has not determined. If there is no connection, personae, at this point in the poem, should be separated from biography.

Contrast with the fulfilled good moment in "By the Fireside" (14:66-68, 18:86-90); there, Robert realizes his elective affinity with Elizabeth (*Comp.*, 54-55, 56, 392-93, 423-24; this appendix, same line numbers).

THE "MOSES" OF MICHAEL ANGELO

1-14 (cont. from *Comp.*, 169)

And who is He that, sculptured in huge stone,
    Sitteth a giant, where no works arrive
    Of straining Art, and hath so prompt and live
The lips, I listen to their very tone?
Moses is He—Ay, that, makes clearly known
    The chin's thick boast, and brow's prerogative
    Of double ray: so did the mountain give
Back to the world that visage, God was grown
Great part of! Such was he when he suspended
    Round him the sounding and vast waters; such
    When he shut sea on sea o'er Mizraïm
And ye, his hordes, a vile calf raised, and bended
    The knee? This Image had ye raised, not much
    Had been your error in adoring Him.

The form for the title and lines 5, 6, and 11 of this sonnet, as given here, corrects that employed in the *Compendium* (169); it is reproduced from *New Poems* (NE, 26). A different indentation of the sestet for the sonnet is given in Pettigrew and Collins (PET, II, 952).

The central image of the sonnet is the substitution of Michelangelo's statue of Moses (*Comp.*, 170, Fig. 88) for the "vile calf" of gold ordered by Aaron and worshipped by the Israelites while Moses was away on Mount Sinai (Exodus, 32:2-6). Had the "Image" of Michelangelo's *Moses*, instead of the Golden Calf, been "raised" and venerated by the Israelites, "not much / Had been. . . error [that is, idolatry] in adoring Him [the *Moses* of Michelangelo]."

MY LAST DUCHESS: FERRARA

48-56 (cont. from *Comp.*, 175-82)

I repeat,

The Count your master's known munificence
Is ample warrant that no just pretense
Of mine for dowry will be disallowed;
Though his fair daughter's self, as I avowed
At starting, is my object. Nay, we'll go
Together down, sir. Notice Neptune, though,
Taming a sea-horse, thought a rarity,
Which Claus of Innsbruck cast in bronze for me!

In the *Compendium* (175-82), I conflate six possible sources for the imaginary Neptune statue in Browning's monologue; the sources are derived from Browning's probable viewing of various art objects during his trip in 1838 throughout northern Italy, Austria, and Germany. To this theory I shall add three statues—all in bronze—and then analyze the symbolic significance of the numerous proposed sources that pertain to the subject of Neptune. Two of the three bronze statues that I am linking to my composite theory portray a German king and an emperor in the Court Church of Innsbruck. They are entered below under *Pippa Passes* as *specific* sources for that poem (Figs. 292, 293), and, although I do not consider them further under the present poem, they strengthen the discussion in the *Compendium* (176) where "Innsbruck," as a foundry site, is advanced as a *general* source. The third bronze statue, which I introduce here, represents Neptune; it is located in Bolzano, Italy.

In a letter dated July 24, 1838, Browning lists the cities of Trieste, Venice, Trent, Innsbruck, and Munich as part of his itinerary during his trip in May and June of 1838, but he does not mention the city of Bolzano (HOO, 3). Bolzano lies between Trent and Innsbruck on the Brenner Pass, however, and Browning could not easily have avoided passing through it. That he did not stay in Bolzano is of course possible, but that he did not at least visit the city is unimaginable, as it is a notable tourist attraction that would have held interest for him. In the Piazza delle Erbe of Bolzano, a famous marketplace, a bronze statue of Neptune forms part of a fountain. It was cast in 1746 by Joachim Pais from a model made by Georg Mayr (BOLZ; Fig. 276). It is one of only two possible sources in my composite theory that answers to Browning's description of a Neptune statue that is "cast in bronze." (The other source is the bronze statuette that was in the Palazzo Rezzonico; it is illustrated by Figure 91 on page 178 of the *Compendium*.)

In Browning scholarship it is almost a commonplace to say that the imaginary statue in the poem represents the over-bearing attitude of Browning's Duke and that just as Neptune is "Taming a seahorse" so, too, in a manner of speaking, the Duke tamed his first wife and will tame the one that he is bargaining for in the poem (BER, 282; BERM, 85). Of the seven models that are advanced in this study as sources for the imaginary Neptune statue—the one here from Bolzano and the six others mentioned in the *Compendium*, pages 175-82—six of the seven models support this traditional interpretation, for, as can be seen in Figures 91, 92, 201, 221, 240 (*Comp.*, pp. 178, 180, 349, 378, 397), and Figure 276 in this appendix, Neptune, in every case, is literally overbearing or standing in various degrees of command. The seventh model, however, Giambattista Tiepolo's painting, *Venice Receives the Homage of Neptune* (*Comp.*, 398, Fig. 241), is unusual as a subject and provides us with a fresh look at the character of Browning's Duke.

In the last three lines of the poem, while the Duke is negotiating for a second wife, he suddenly calls attention to Neptune in the form of an art object. This juxtaposition of bargaining and referring to Neptune implies the mercantile side of the Duke's character; the way Tiepolo's painting acts as a sub-image to the text reinforces this idea. Tiepolo's Neptune, reclining with his cornucopia of riches from the sea, calls to mind the former days of Venetian glory when yearly the Doge threw a ring into the ocean to wed with the sea, to symbolize the rule of the Doges over the sea or, to follow the metaphor of the painting, to symbolize homage to Venice by Neptune—by the sea, by maritime commerce. (Also, see under "A Toccata of Galuppi's" in the *Compendium*, pages 369-70, and in this appendix above under the same poem and Figure 299 for more about the ring ceremony.) In the same spirit of commerce, the model Duke of Ferrara in the poem, Alphonso d'Este II, married Lucrezia de'Medici followed by Barbara of Austria, for, as history tells us, both wives brought to their marriages large dowries (DEVA, 108, 109). Barbara of Austria's ample dowry is even specifically acknowledged when Browning's Duke mentions "The Count your master's known munificence."

But how can one justify Tiepolo's painting as a model

when Browning's text specifies a statue and not a painting? This discrepancy is justified, I think, by the importance of another proposed source in Venice, the Sansovino statue of Neptune at the top of the Giant Staircase in the Ducal Palace of Venice (*Comp.*, 349, Fig. 201, left and right). The Neptune statue surmounting the Giant Staircase establishes the Ducal Palace as part of the setting in keeping with the text "Nay, we'll go / Together down, sir. Notice Neptune, though"; the Este Castle of Ferrara, the reader will recall, is the other proposed model for the composite setting (*Comp.*, 173-75, Fig. 90). Tiepolo's painting, then, being housed in the Ducal Palace of Venice, relates to the composite model setting in Ferrara and Venice: Tiepolo's painting and the collateral settings of the Este Castle and the Ducal Palace of Venice suggest that both the Este family of Ferrara and the Doges of Venice were concerned with the business of marriage, whether it involved real dowries or a symbolic wedding with maritime commerce.

OLD PICTURES IN FLORENCE

13:97-98, 101 (cont. from *Comp.*, 186, 187, 189, 193)

> You would fain be kinglier, say, than I am?
> Even so, you will not sit like Theseus.
> . . .
> You're wroth—can you slay your snake like Apollo?

Compare "Theseus" here with the same statue characterized as "godlike hardship" in Keats's sonnet "On Seeing the Elgin Marbles" (line 4). In both texts the perfectibility of Greek art underscores the imperfectibility of man, but Keats stops at man's mortality, whereas Browning goes on to his Doctrine of the Imperfect (also see above under "Cleon," 82, 88-94, para. two).

Browning's reference to the statue of Theseus may also have been influenced by William Hazlitt's essay "Flaxman's Lectures on Sculpture." Alberti advances this idea and quotes Hazlitt's comments on the statue (HAZL, XVI, 353):

> . . . in the fragment of the Theseus, the whole is melted into one impression like wax; there is all the flexibility, the malleableness of flesh; there is the same alternate tension and relaxation. . . .

In particular, Alberti thinks that the phrase "alternate tension and relaxation" may have informed the implied movement of muscles in the line "you will not sit like Theseus" (AL, 128-29; *Comp.*, 187, Fig. 95).

The line "You're wroth—can you slay your snake like Apollo" I assign in the *Compendium* to the *Omphalos Apollo* (pp. 186, 189, Fig. 97, p. 193). But this attribution, based on a note by Browning, is only partly correct, for Browning's note about the statue (*Comp.*, 193) also mentions "Apollo the snakeslayer. . . the god of the Belvedere," which is no doubt the famous *Apollo Belvedere*, once in the Belvedere courtyard of the Vatican and now in the Museo Pio-Clementino (COOKE, 220; BER, 291; AL, 130; Fig. 278).

26:201-02 (cont. from *Comp.*, 194, 433-34)

> Not that I expect the great Bigordi,
> Nor Sandro to hear me. . . .

The description in the *Compendium* of the competition between "Sandro" Botticelli and the "great Bigordi," more familiarly known as Domenico Ghirlandaio, is certainly recorded in Vasari's *Lives*, but the painting that Botticelli did for the Church of Ognissanti is not a St. Jerome; rather, it is the fresco titled *St. Augustine in His Study* (EISE, in conversation, August, 1992; VAS, II, 173; AL, 156; *Comp.*, 433-34). The fresco by Ghirlandaio, *St. Jerome in His Study* (Fig. 280), is on pier in the church (*Comp.*, 198, Fig. 103; Map F:7G) facing the Botticelli pier fresco of St. Augustine (Fig. 281).

The competition between Botticelli and Ghirlandaio, involving paintings with similar media, subjects, and settings—frescoes of scholarly saints sitting in their studies—is a prominent example of the development of individualism through rivalry in the Renaissance artist.

Also, above under "Cleon," lines 82, 88-94, the conglomerate of pictures on the pavement of the Duomo of Siena represents artistic individualism during the Renaissance period.

26:205-08 (cont. from *Comp.*, 194, 195)

> But are you too fine, Taddeo Gaddi,
> To grant me a taste of your intonaco,
> Some Jerome that seeks the heaven with a sad eye?
> Not a churlish saint, Lorenzo Monaco?

Alberti puts forth the side panels from Lorenzo Monaco's *San Benedetto Altarpiece* as possible sources for Browning's line "Not a churlish saint, Lorenzo Monaco?" The side panels are each titled *Adoring Saints* and are each comprised of eight saints (EISEN, 138-45). The panels were obtained by the National Gallery of London in 1848 (cat. nos. 215 and 216; Fig. 283) and could have been seen by Browning during his return to London in 1851, four years before the publishing of "Old Pictures in Florence." Alberti interprets Don Lorenzo's saints as "churlish" because some of them are designed with V-shaped lines over the noses to indicate frowning (see the detail in Fig. 283). Unfortunately for Alberti's hypothesis, as she admits, the panels were attributed to Taddeo Gaddi and not Lorenzo Monaco at the time Browning could have seen them in 1851 (DAVI, 308, 309, n. 13; EISEN, 139). But Alberti speculates that Browning might have recognized the style of Don Lorenzo and reflected his attribution of the painting to Don Lorenzo in his poem (AL, 17, 174). What Alberti does not mention, however, that I think strengthens her case, is that the name "Taddeo Gaddi" is given in Browning's text within a few lines of the name "Lorenzo Monaco," and this proximity suggests that Browning might have been making some association between the two artists. The association is further strengthened by the probability of Browning's reading about Don Lorenzo in his own copy of the 1550 Florentine edition of Vasari's *Lives*. Lorenzo Monaco's style is deeply influenced by the Gaddesque tradition stemming from Taddeo Gaddi to his son Agnolo (EISE, in conversation, September, 1993; VASARI, 215-18).

Marvin Eisenberg's identification of "Some Jerome that seeks the heaven with a sad eye" is presented in the *Compendium* (194, 195) and illustrated in this appendix (Fig. 282).

27:213-216 (cont. from *Comp.*, 194, 195, 435, 436)

> No Virgin by him the somewhat petty,
>   Of finical touch and tempera crumbly—
> Could not Alesso Baldovinetti
>   Contribute so much, I ask him humbly?

Figure 270 features the "Virgin" in Baldovinetti's fresco of the Nativity. The painting, as part of a complex of frescoes in the Cloister of the Madonna, or atrium, of the Church of the Santissima Annunziata in Florence (Map F:6I,7I), is also implied in the citation under "Andrea del Sarto," lines 259-63, which is entered both in the *Compendium* (30, 420) and above in this appendix.

PARLEYING WITH CHRISTOPHER SMART

3:40-44

> There fronted me the Rafael Mother-Maid,
> Never to whom knelt votarist in shrine
> By Nature's bounty helped, by Art's divine
> More varied—beauty with magnificence—
> Than this. . . .

The "Rafael Mother-Maid" could be the painter's *Madonna del Granduca*, in the Pitti Palace, Florence (*Comp.*, 210, Fig. 111; Map F:9G). In "One Word More," section 3, line 23, a Madonna by Raphael is described as "Her, that visits Florence in a vision," and Browning, in a letter to Rolfe, confirms this line as a reference to the *Madonna del Granduca* (*Comp.*, 206):

> The Madonna at Florence is that called del Granduca, which represents her 'as appearing to a votary in a vision'—so say the describers; it is in the earlier manner, and very beautiful. . . .

I make the connection between the *Madonna del Granduca* in the present text and "One Word More" through the words "votarist" and "votary." These words, according to the *Oxford English Dictionary*, are synonymous, in that they both mean one who venerates bound by religious vows. In "Parleying with Christopher Smart," Browning places the "Rafael Mother-Maid" with a "knelt votarist in shrine," that is, in a shrine or chapel with one of the faithful in supplication before an image of a Madonna by Raphael. In his letter to Rolfe, Browning identifies the *Madonna del Granduca* in "One Word More" as that Madonna by Raphael which "describers" say is "appearing to a votary in a vision." The votary or votarist is envisioning the Madonna rather than kneeling before her, but the effect is the same: he or she is venerating, bound by religious vows, the Virgin Mary in a painting by Raphael.

Another case involving the same painting is elaborated upon under *The Ring and the Book* in the *Compendium* (304, 305-306) and below under the same poem (VI.400-06, 667-73, 913-14).

PARLEYING WITH FRANCIS FURINI

2:76-96

> Yes, I assure you: he [Furini] would paint—not men
> Merely—a pardonable fault—but when
> He had to deal with—oh, not mother Eve
> Alone, permissibly in Paradise
> Naked and unashamed,—but dared achieve
> Dreadful distinction, at soul-safety's price,
> By also painting women—(why the need?)
> Just as God made them: there, you have the truth!
> Yes, rosed from top to toe in flush of youth,
> One foot upon the moss-fringe, would some Nymph
> Try, with its venturous fellow, if the lymph
> Were chillier than the slab-stepped fountain-edge;
> The while a-heap her garments on its ledge
> Of boulder lay within hand's easy reach,
> —No one least kid-skin cast around her! Speech
> Shrinks from enumerating case and case
> Of—were it but Diana at the chase,
> With tunic tucked discreetly hunting-high!
> No, some Queen Venus set our necks awry,
> Turned faces from the painter's all-too-frank
> Triumph of flesh!

The references in this passage to "Eve," "some Nymph," "Diana," and "Queen Venus" indicate subjects of paintings of nudes by Francesco Furini. These subjects are either mentioned by Baldinucci in his *Notizie*, the acknowledged source for this poem, or they are presented as follows in Pilkington's *Dictionary of Painters*, which was also known to Browning (BALD, IV, 629-44; PIL, 203; GRI, 15n):

> He [Furini] was particularly fond of designing naked figures, as in those he showed the utmost delicacy; and he principally chose to paint those subjects in which they could be introduced with elegance and propriety; such as Adam and Eve, Lot and his Daughters, Noah's Drunkenness, and such like; or similar subjects from poetical history, as, the Death of Adonis, Diana and other Nymphs bathing, the Judgment of Paris, &c.

Two of the paintings indicated by the subjects described in the text at hand can be specifically identified and located. Browning no doubt saw Furini's *Adam and Eve in Earthly Paradise* in the Pitti Palace while residing in Florence (Fig. 285; Map F:9G); the emphasis in the text on the title of the painting and the unabashed nude pose of Eve, on "Eve. . . in Paradise / Naked and unashamed," confirms this attribution. What Pilkington calls the "Death of Adonis" probably combines with what Browning terms "Queen Venus" in order to form Furini's *Venus Mourning the Death of Adonis*, in the Budapest Gallery. As can be seen in Figure 284, the indecorous position of the legs of the grieving Venus gives rise to the exclamation in Browning's text:

> . . . some Queen Venus set our necks awry,
> Turned faces from the painter's all-too-frank
> Triumph of flesh!

The paintings of nudes by Furini that Rowena Fowler has observed do not support Pilkington's assessment that Furini's treatment of the nude is rendered with "utmost delicacy. . . elegance and propriety"; rather, she finds them titillating (FOW, 43). Certainly Browning, by emphatically calling attention to the indecorousness of Furini's painting of Venus, "the painter's all-too-frank / Triumph of flesh!" points up the exception to Pilkington's claim and begins a notable argument in the poem: the issue of nudity in art as a vehicle of beauty opposed to the exploitation of sexuality. The argument is taken up below under the next entry.

Another painting of the female nude by Furini, his *Andromeda*, which is listed by Baldinucci (BALD, IV, 632) but not by Pilkington, is noted under this poem in the *Compendium* (221).

3:152-60

>   What—not merely wake
> Our pity that suppressed concupiscence—
> A satyr masked as matron—makes pretence
> To the coarse blue-fly's instinct—can perceive
> No better reason why she should exist—
> —God's lily-limbed and blushrose-bosomed Eve—
> Than as a hot-bed for the sensualist
> To fly-blow with his fancies, make pure stuff
> Breed him back filth—this were not crime enough?

From the combined identifications of other scholars and myself, the line "God's lily-limbed and blushrose-bosomed Eve" appears to be an allusion to an unspecified conflation of sources; the allusion seems to be based on two nude paintings of Eve, one nude plaster sculpture on the subject of Eve, and a collateral source to the sculpture of Eve, which is a nude bronze statue of Dryope. One of the paintings of Eve DeVane advances as Francesco Furini's *Adam and Eve in Earthly Paradise* (DEVAN, 180, n. 39; Fig. 285). For a more specific mention of Furini's painting of Eve, see this poem above under section 2, lines 76-96.

Porter and Clarke identify the other painting as Michelangelo's fresco the *Creation of Eve*, on the vault of the Sistine Chapel in the Vatican (POR, XII, 350). Michelangelo's Eve is clearly visualized farther on in section 3 here, in lines 180-81 (*Comp.*, 221, 223, Fig. 120):

> His Eve low bending took the privilege
> Of life from what our eyes saw—God's own palm. . . .

An additional description of the same fresco by Michelangelo occurs below under "Parleying with Charles Avison" (8:232-34, 248).

I nominate the sculpture of Eve possibly alluded to in the passage under consideration; it is Pen Browning's *Eve after Temptation*. Kelley and Coley catalogue it as a life-sized plaster statue fashioned around 1882, and Figure 289 reproduces the statue from a photograph housed in the Armstrong Browning Library, in Waco, Texas. The original statue was acquired by Antonio Morassutti, of Montebelluno, Italy, in 1912, from the Pen Browning estate at Asolo (KEL, 544, item K75).

I also put forth the collateral source to Pen Browning's nude plaster statue of Eve, his nude bronze statue of Dryope, now in a private collection in England (KEL, 544, item K76; Fig. 286, right). One reason for this proposal is that the subjects of Eve and Dryope were conceivably interchangeable in Browning's mind; evidence for this is presented below under "Parleying with Gerard de Lairesse" (5:116-26, para. 4). Further support for Pen's bronze *Dryope* as a collateral source follows from the historical context for the passage under discussion. DeVane points out that the phrase "A satyr masked as matron" is an allusion to the critic John Calcot Horsley, who anonymously signed one of his published letters as "a British matron." Horsley, a painter, treasurer and unofficial publicist of the Royal Academy, and patron of the Burlington House, brought about the refusal to exhibit Pen's nude bronze statue of Dryope in an 1884 exhibition at the Burlington House (DEVA, 513-14).

Browning was no doubt sensitive to this rejection because

of his involvement in the Dryope project. The subject of Dryope for a work of art, DeVane reports, was suggested to Pen by his father, and DeVane believes that Browning, in turn, got the idea from the passage about Dryope in *The Art of Painting*, which is entered as a source below under "Parleying with Gerard de Lairesse," section 5, lines 116-26 (DEVAN, 182, n. 45, 183, n. 53). But DeVane does not point out that Lairesse employs the female nude in his *visual* version of the Dryope myth (Fig. 290); had DeVane mentioned this and recognized the possible extent of Lairesse's influence on Browning, DeVane would have strengthened his hypothesis, as I am trying to do, and could have maintained that Browning might even have recommended to his son the nude treatment of Dryope that we see in Figure 286, as possibly suggested to Browning by the nudity in Figure 290.

The historical context for the passage at hand indicates that Browning was close to the work of his son and was aesthetically committed to his son's rendering of the female nude. De-Vane maintains that the general parallel Browning makes in "Parleying with Francis Furini" is that Horsley objected to Pen Browning's depiction of the female nude just as Baldinucci was averse to Furini's painting of nudes (DEVAN, 183; PET, II, 1111). The specific implication in the present text is that just as Baldinucci denounced Furini's nude painting of Eve, Horsley would have condemned Pen's nude plaster sculpture of Eve, and Horsley would have done so in the same manner that he effected the banishment of Pen's nude bronze statue of Dryope. Browning's purpose in conflating the proposed nude versions of Eve by Furini, Michelangelo, and his son, Pen, is to show that Horsley's opposition to Pen's depiction of the female nude is absurd in light of either the lesser nudes of Furini or the greater of Michelangelo. Horsley manifests "suppressed concupiscence"; he is a "sensualist" who projects his own sexual feelings into an artist's rendering of nudes and assumes that all nude art, whether Pen Browning's, Furini's, or even Michelangelo's, is, as expressed toward the end of section three, "lust-born," that "mere lust / Inspired the artist."

Another rendering of the nude by Pen Browning that applies to the topic just discussed is his *Joan of Arc and the Kingfisher* (Fig. 287), which is entered in the *Compendium* (221, 223) and developed below under the next entry (11:601-07). There, in fairness to Baldinucci and Horsley, the issue raised above under this poem concerning Furini's nudes (2:76-96) is applied to the nudes of Pen Browning: are they provocative or representative of beauty?

11:601-07 (cont. from *Comp.*, 221, 223)

> *Now as she fain would bathe, one even-tide,*
> *God's maid, this Joan, from the pool's edge she spied*
> *The fair blue bird clowns call the Fisher-king:*
> *And "'Las, [sic] sighed she, [sic] my Liege is such a thing*
> *As thou, lord but of one poor lonely place*
> *Out of his whole wide France: were mine the grace*
> *To set my Dauphin free as thou, blue bird!"*

Browning's response to the critics of his son's painting *Joan of Arc and the Kingfisher* (Fig. 287; illustrated as *Nude Study* in WAR, 91) is set forth in a letter dated May 12, 1886 (HOO 247; DEVAN, 183; DEVA, 514; PET, II, 1112): "I am ashamed at the objection taken by some of the critics to the Eve-like simplicity of Pen's peasant-girl. . . ." But Rowena Fowler points out that Browning, too fraught with defending his son's treatment of the nude, overlooks what is sensual to the voyeur in Pen's painting: a counterpoised Joan of Arc who displays herself rather than "Eve-like simplicity" (FOW, 44).

The conflicting views of the nude in art as a form of beauty or lasciviousness are also treated above under this poem (2:76-96 and 3:152-60) and below under "Parleying with Gerard de Lairesse" (5:116-26). The championing of Pen's painting by his father is further considered below under *The Ring and the Book* (I.38, 45-49).

PARLEYING WITH GERARD DE LAIRESSE

3:71-80

> . . .
> In that old sepulchre by lightning split,
> Whereof the lid bore carven,—any dolt
> Imagines why,—Jove's very thunderbolt:
> You who could straight perceive, by glance at it,
> This tomb must needs be Phaeton's! In a trice,
> Confirming that conjecture, close on hand,
> Behold, half out, half in the ploughed-up sand,
> A chariot-wheel explained its bolt-device:
> What other than the Chariot of the Sun
> Ever let drop the like?

In Gerard de Lairesse's treatise, *The Art of Painting in All Its Branches*, Lairesse takes his reader on an imaginary walk in order to show him what is fit as a subject for painting. In this passage Browning's description of Phaethon's tomb is a poetic account of Lairesse's prosaic one (DEVAN, 242, n. 74).

What DeVane does not reproduce, however, is Figure 277, an illustration from *The Art of Painting* that shows Zeus holding a thunderbolt—"Jove's very thunderbolt"—that can be imagined, as "lightning, split[ting]" Phaethon's tomb and carving on it a "bolt-device" (LAI, Plate XXXIX).

Phaethon's attempt to drive the "Chariot of the Sun" out of Olympus must have appealed to Browning's sense of daring failure. Compare Browning's use of the Doctrine of the Imperfect above under "A Grammarian's Funeral," lines 31-34. There, Browning's grammarian is characterized as Apollo, the sun-god, in the act of ascending to Olympus.

5:116-26

> How were it could I mingle false with true,
> Boast, with the sights I see, your vision too?
> Advantage would it prove or detriment
> If I saw double? Could I gaze intent
> On Dryope plucking the blossoms red,
> As you, whereat her lote-tree writhed and bled,
> Yet lose no gain, no hard fast wide-awake
> Having and holding nature for the sake
> Of nature only—nymph and lote-tree thus
> Gained by the loss of fruit not fabulous,
> Apple of English homesteads.

The literary source for this vignette depicting the story of Dryope is taken from Gerard de Lairesse's *The Art of Painting in All Its Branches* and is given in part by DeVane (LAI, 239; DEVAN, 230, n. 48):

> I exhibit the subject. . . in a delightful valley (according to the testimony of the poet [Ovid]), planted with myrtles, and encompassed by a brook. In the middle of the piece, I place, as the principal, the tree *Lotos*, full of red blossoms and thickly leaved. From this tree *Dryope* broke off the sprig. . . .

DeVane, however, does not include the illustration that is indicated in the full text of the opening clause by Lairesse. Without the ellipsis the clause reads: "I exhibit the subject (*see Plate LIV*) in a delightful valley." The parenthetical words "(see Plate LIV)" are italicized by me in order to emphasize what DeVane omits. Plate LIV from *The Art of Painting* is reproduced in Figure 290, and it corresponds with Lairesse's detailed verbal description of the scene (LAI, 239-42). To my knowledge, this illustration and the two others reproduced from Lairesse's book as Figures 277 and 291 have not been previously used in Browning studies.

The thematic significance of Browning's text at hand is set forth by Robert Langbaum (LAN, 160):

> In rejecting myth in "Parleying with Gerard de Lairesse," Browning asks whether he would do better to tell two stories— to repeat the old myth through realistically apprehended modern circumstances, repeat the myth of Dryope plucking the lotus blossoms through the story of an English girl plucking "fruit not fabulous" but "Apple of English homesteads." "Advantage would it prove or detriment / If I saw double?"

As an expansion of what Professor Langbaum calls "repeat[ing] the old myth through realistically apprehended modern circumstances," three lines of thought should be explored.

First, to recapitulate from the preceding poem, "Parleying with Frances Furini," section 3, lines 152-60, the issue over whether the nude in art is lascivious or beautiful arises concerning three nude versions of Eve, including a plaster statue by Pen Browning, his *Eve after Temptation* (Fig. 289); the issue is further developed in regard to a nude bronze statue of Dryope by Pen (Fig. 286, right). In opposition to Filippo Baldinucci's and John Calcot Horsley's objection to the nude, Robert Browning's position in the "Furini" poem is that nude art is not lustful, that "God's best of beauteous and magnificent / Revealed to earth [is] the naked female form" (Par, 3:142-43). Under the citation at hand, an echo of the debate over nude art is heard through the words "Dryope" and "Apple" because of the implication in the "Furini" poem of the nudity of Pen Browning's bronze statue of Dryope, which Horsley condemned, and the depiction of an apple in Pen's nude plaster statue of Eve. Robert Browning, in the present text, by substituting an "Apple" for the lotus "blossoms red," enables us to view the Dryope myth with a "vision. . . double," with not only a literal repetition of the Dryope story but also with cross-allusions to Pen Browning's representations of Dryope and Eve as sculptured nude forms.

Moreover, Pen's bronze *Dryope* might have been associated by Browning with Pen's *Eve after Temptation* because of the interchangeability of their titles. To demonstrate this point I must discuss Pen's plaster statue of Dryope, which is not to be confused with his Dryope bronze. Kelley, Coley, and Townsend catalogue Pen's plaster *Dryope* by its alternate title, *Eve* (KELLE, 30, item 74; Fig. 286, left, with the bronze on the right). This listing is documented by Fanny Browning, who wrote on the back of a photograph of the plaster version of the Dryope statue, "Dryope sometimes called Eve" (the photograph belongs to The Browning Institute, care of Eton College; the documentation and a copy of the photograph were kindly provided by Betty A. Coley). Since the plaster statue of Dryope is apparently a model for the bronze version (compare the statues in Fig. 286), I conclude that *both* statues can be alternately called *Eve*. The significance of this conclusion is further developed at the end of this note.

Second, in Browning's double vision or double metaphor or, to be precise, double synecdoche, the apple is utilized to express the theme of "holding nature for the sake / Of nature only," that is, holding up nature as real fruit, "fruit not fabulous." The apple in Pen Browning's *Eve after Temptation* is of course legendary if not fabulous, but Pen also rendered fruit realistically in still-life pictures. In particular, I call attention to the apple depicted prominently in Pen's undated watercolor titled *Still Life of Fruits and Vegetables* (KEL, 548, item K117; Fig. 288, in color; reproduced in black and white in WAR, 84, as *Still-Life Study*). Furthermore, the "Apple of English homesteads" in Browning's text not only associates with Pen's watercolor but also with Pen himself; Pen, though born in Italy and offered Italian citizenship by Florentine authorities, was always an Englishman in Browning's eyes (WAR, 42; KO, 152, 154).

Third, from the reading of Rowena Fowler's article "Browning's Nudes," it occurs to me that the two foregoing lines of thought merge into a synthesis. Professor Fowler maintains that Browning deflects—or transfers—the problem of nudity by displacing the naked female body into landscape (FOW, 45). A case in point, in addition to the ones that Fowler gives, can be made here. Browning implies the transfer of the apple in Pen's *Eve after Temptation* to Pen's *Still Life of Fruits and Vegetables*, and Pen's plaster and bronze sculptures of Dryope as Eve can each be imagined—with or without an apple—being transferred to his still-life study. I say "imagined—with or without an apple" because Pen's bronze and plaster statues of Dryope or Eve do not show her holding an apple, as we see in Pen's *Eve after Temptation*. But all three sculptures depict the biblical serpent, and our eyes *look* for the apple associated with the serpent. Or, to take a larger view, again there is synecdoche: Pen's three sculptured nudes of Eve—or Dryope as Eve—are displaced into one still-life apple.

Below under *The Ring and the Book* (I.1-4, 15-17, paragraphs 4-6), a lily is described being transferred from one painting to another.

6:163-65

> The rose? No rose unless it disentwine
> From Venus' wreath the while she bends to kiss
> Her deathly love?

Figure 291 reproduces Plate XVIII from Gerard de Lairesse's *The Art of Painting*. The text accompanying the plate reads as follows (LAI, 77):

> The story is, *Venus*, inconsoleable [sic] for the death of her dear *Adonis*; even the aid of *Cupid* fails, whose bow, arrows and extinguished torch, nay her beloved garland of roses, she tramples under foot; *Mars*, though secretly pleased at the adventure, however pretends to sympathize with her in her sorrow, but in vain; for she slights his offers, and pushes him from her; she rests on the tomb of her lover, wherein either his body is deposited, or (according to the custom of the country) his ashes are kept in the urn. . . .

Correspondences between Lairesse's account of his illustration and Browning's text concern the action involving the "rose" and the mode by which Venus "bends" her body. The rose can easily "disentwine" because, as appears in the lower illustration in Figure 291, the "garland of roses, she [Venus] tramples under foot." Venus does not bend to "kiss / Her deathly love," but, in both the upper and lower illustrations, she bends and "rests on the tomb of her lover," Adonis, whose "body" or whose "ashes are kept in the urn." Browning, further on in the poem, appears to identify the contents of the urn as ashes, for in section 14, lines 392 and 393, he states:

> The dead Greek lore lies buried in the urn
> Where who seeks fire finds ashes.

As a thematic summary of his rejection of "Greek lore,"
Browning alludes to Adonis, as represented by the "ashes" in the
"urn," and to Prometheus (see the entry immediately below),
whose "fire" cannot be found.

8:188-98

> . . .
> Circled with flame there yawned a sudden rift
> I' the rock-face, and I saw a form erect
> Front and defy the outrage, while—as checked,
> Chidden, beside him dauntless in the drift—
> Cowered a heaped creature, wing and wing outspread
> In deprecation o'er the crouching head
> Still hungry for the feast foregone awhile.
> O thou, of scorn's unconquerable smile,
> Was it when this—Jove's feathered fury—slipped
> Gore-glutted from the heart's core whence he ripped—
> This eagle-hound. . . .

Browning's version of an imaginary walk, in contrast to
Lairesse's walk to find appropriate subjects for paintings, begins
with a word-picture of Prometheus and the eagle of Zeus. The
literary sources of this scene owe much to Elizabeth Barrett
Browning's translation of *Prometheus Bound* (POR, XII, 355, n.
196; DEVAN, 245), to Shelley's *Prometheus Unbound* (RYA,
219), and to the original play by Aeschylus (OR, 356, n. 2). For an
illustration as a collateral source to the literary ones, we can turn
to Lairesse's *The Art of Painting*, in which, in Figure 277, we see
Zeus posed with a thunderbolt and his eagle, "Jove's feathered
fury" (LAI, Plate XXXIX). Figure 277 also serves as a possible
source for the passage cited from this poem above under section
3, lines 71-80.

9:230-45

> Moon-maid in heaven above and, here below,
> Earth's huntress-queen? I note the garb succinct
> Saving from smirch that purity of snow
> From breast to knee—snow's self with just the tint
> Of the apple-blossom's heart-blush. Ah, the bow
> Slack-strung her fingers grasp, where, ivory-linked
> Horn curving blends with horn, a moonlike pair
> Which mimic the brow's crescent sparkling so—
> As if a star's live restless fragment winked
> Proud yet repugnant, captive in such hair!
> What hope along the hillside, what far bliss

Lets the crisp hair-plaits fall so low they kiss
Those lucid shoulders? Must a morn so blithe
Needs have its sorrow when the twang and hiss
Tell that from out thy sheaf one shaft makes writhe
Its victim, thou unerring Artemis?

This word-picture in Browning's version of Lairesse's walk, which depicts "Artemis," or Diana, "Moon-maid in heaven above and, here below, / Earth's huntress-queen," is a description of a painting that I have already identified in the *Compendium* in another context. Under *The Ring and the Book*, Book VII, lines 186-96 (*Comp.* pp. 314, 402, Fig. 245, p. 445), I give Giambattista Tiepolo's *Diana*, in the Dulwich Picture Gallery, as the source for one of the scenes in an imaginary tapestry:

"Tisbe, that is you,
With half-moon on your hair-knot, spear in hand,
Flying, but no wings, only the great scarf
Blown to a bluish rainbow at your back:
Call off your hound and leave the stag alone!"

In the present passage I detect new details that can be discerned in the same painting. Diana's "garb succinct" is white and pinkish, "snow's self with just the tint / Of the apple-blossom's heart-blush." The crescent curves in the horns of each deer match with each other, that is, the "ivory-linked / Horn curving blends with horn, a moon-like pair." The pairs of curving crescents in the horns of the deer resemble Diana's hairpiece, in that they "mimic the brow's crescent sparkling so. . . captive in such hair." And the "crisp hair-plaits fall so low they kiss / Those lucid shoulders." One discrepancy, however, should be pointed out. In the passage from *The Ring and the Book*, Diana is holding what appears to be a "spear in hand," but in the present citation "the bow / Slack-strung her fingers grasp." The logical object that Diana grasps is a bow and not a spear because, with the other hand, she holds a quiver, a "sheaf," from which she takes out an arrow, "one shaft." Nevertheless, it is understandable how Browning, in recalling the painting from memory, could envision the slackened bow in the shape of a spear, especially since the bow, in its loosened condition, *looks* like a spear (*Comp.*, 402, Fig. 245; the color identifications noted at the beginning of this discussion were corroborated in conversation with G. A. Waterfield, Director of the Dulwich Picture Gallery, and also with the help of Dr. Ann Sumner, Assistant Curator of the gallery).

DeVane insists that descriptions of the moon in Browning's poetry after "One Word More"—to quote DeVane's own words—"always" or "almost always" represent Elizabeth Barrett Browning (DEVA, p. 278, n. 63, pp. 490, 504). (The facts above under "By the Fireside," 14:66-68, 18:86-90, suggest that the moon imagery actually begins with "By the Fireside" two years earlier.) Included among DeVane's examples of his claim is the depiction of the moon in "Parleying with Daniel Bartoli," section 17, lines 285-86, in which "the cloud that thrust between / Him [Browning] and effulgence [the moon, Elizabeth]" is interpreted as Louisa, Lady Ashburton, who temporarily obscured or interfered with Browning's memory of Elizabeth (DEVA, 504). In the passage under present scrutiny, the moon, through mythology, takes a more active part in the symbolism. Diana or "Artemis," the "Moon-maid" as "Earth's huntress-queen," is the personification of the memory of Elizabeth Barrett Browning, whose "shaft" makes her "victim," Lady Ashburton, "writhe."

Related to this interpretation and the Browning-Ashburton debacle is the flower imagery of daisies and tulips analyzed as part of the proposed setting of Elizabeth's grave site implied at the end of this poem; the analysis is given below under section 16, lines 426-34. Also see above under "Flute-Music, with an Accompaniment," lines 46-48.

11:321-34

> I see!
> Bent on a battle, two vast powers agree
> This present and no after-contest ends
> One or the other's grasp at rule in reach
> Over the race of man—host fronting host,
> As statue statue fronts—wrath-molten each,
> Solidified by hate,—earth halved almost,
> To close once more in chaos. Yet two shapes
> Show prominent, each from the universe
> Of minions round about him, that disperse
> Like cloud-obstruction when a bolt escapes.
> Who flames first? Macedonian, is it thou?
> Ay, and who fronts thee, King Darius, drapes
> His form with purple, fillet-folds his brow.

As another word-picture in Browning's version of a walk with Gerard de Lairesse, this vignette, I submit, is vividly modelled after the famous mosaic in the Archeological Museum of

Naples, *The Battle of Isso.* Figure 297, top, illustrates details in
the mosaic that correspond with Browning's text: "two shapes /
Show prominent, each from the universe / Of minions round
about him, that disperse / Like cloud-obstruction when a bolt
escapes";   Alexander, the "Mace-donian," and "King Darius"
stand out from their armies (Alexander is on the far left in profile facing Darius) as if "statue statue fronts"; and the headdress
and purple color of the gar-ments on the Persian king correspond, as can be seen in Figure 297, bottom, in that "King Darius
. . . drapes / His form with purple, [with] fillet-folds [over] his
brow."
      Browning very likely saw the mosaic when he visited
Naples in 1844; the opening exclamatory words of the text—"I
see!"—invite the reader to share with Browning that probable
concrete experience.

16:426-34

                                        . . .
          Dance, yellows and whites and reds,
          Lead your gay orgy, leaves, stalks, heads
          Astir with the wind in the tulip-beds!

          There's sunshine; scarcely a wind at all
          Disturbs starved grass and daisies small
          On a certain mound by a churchyard wall.

          Daisies and grass be my heart's bedfellows
          On the mound wind spares and sunshine mellows:
          Dance you, reds and whites and yellows!

Mary Ellis Gibson concurs with DeVane that this passage refers
to the grave of Elizabeth Barrett Browning (DEVA, 519; GIB, 240).
Elizabeth's tomb (*Comp.*, 88, Fig. 37) rests "On a certain mound"
that is within the walls—not "by a churchyard wall"—of the
Protestant Cemetery in Piazza Donatello, Florence. The cemetery takes the form of an oval hill, and Elizabeth's tomb lies on
the top part of the hill or mound.
      The images in the text of the "tulip-beds" and the "daisies
small" pick up the flower symbolism Browning uses in *Fifine at
the Fair* to express Don Juan's disloyalty to Elvire and Browning's betrayal of the memory of Elizabeth. The end of section 4
in *Fifine* reads:

                                  . . . a slow caravan,
          A chimneyed house on wheels; so shyly-sheathed, began

> To broaden out the bud which, bursting unaware,
> Now takes away our breath, queen-tulip of the Fair!

Section 18 concludes:

> We gather daisy meek, or maiden violet:
> I think it is Elvire we love, and not Fifine.

In the first quotation the brilliant "queen-tulip of the Fair" un-doubtedly represents Fifine, and in the second citation the "daisy meek" is obviously "Elvire," whom the uncertain Don Juan "*think[s]*" he loves rather than "Fifine" [italics mine].

At the biographical level, a number of scholars are agreed that in *Fifine at the Fair* Don Juan is a persona or masque for Browning, Elvire for Elizabeth Barrett Browning, and Fifine for Louisa, Lady Ashburton; and this agreement is in the face of William Whitla's criticism that such personae for Browning and Lady Ashburton do not suit their characters (RAY, 587-99; DEVA, 367-68; MELC, 186; WHIT, 36; IRV, 468; RYA, 61; SOU, 14-16; PET, II, 975-76). But given the validity of the symbolism of the tulip and the daisy in *Fifine at the Fair* and encouraged by the biographical title and substance of DeVane's seminal study *Browning's Parleyings, the Autobiography of a Mind* (DEVAN), I take a modified position, through the implication of Elizabeth's tomb and the flower imagery here, and perceive a recollection of the Browning-Ashburton fiasco; my emphasis, however, is on Robert's ultimate loyalty to rather than his temporary betrayal of the memory of Elizabeth:

> Daisies and grass be my heart's bedfellows
> On the mound wind spares and sunshine mellows. . . .

The "Daisies. . . On the mound" of the Florentine Protes-tant Cemetery in Piazza Donatello are reinforced by a series of designs that pass for daisies alternating with fleur-de-lis devices on the frieze of the entablature under the lid of Elizabeth's tomb; passable daisy designs ornament the capitals of each of the columns supporting the tomb (*Comp.*, 88, Fig. 37). There are no tulips, it should be noted, decorating the tomb. The presence of daisies in permanent stone suggests an intimacy that real, ephemeral daisies cannot quite represent: Robert's enduring memories of Elizabeth adorn her tomb as if they were his "heart's [Elizabeth's] bedfellows."

Michael Meredith calls to my attention the fact that Browning, during the late 1880's, had before him in his study in De Vere Gardens a photograph of Elizabeth's tomb (KEL, 491, item H253, Plate 32). Also, Browning had another photograph of the tomb, which, in 1867, he sent to James Martin (KEL, 491, item H255). Figure 37 in the *Compendium*, page 88, shows one long side of the tomb; the photograph that Browning sent to James Martin gives a view of the other long side (MER, p. 51, Plate 25, p. 84, item 56; also see ORMO, Fig. 100). Browning, we know, never returned to Florence to see the tomb in person (*Comp.*, 89), but he could have seen the decorative motifs—the daisy designs and the fleur-de-lis devices—on the tomb in the photograph sent to James Martin and, possibly, in the one from De Vere Gardens.

The daisy in regard to Elizabeth's tomb is further developed above under "Flute-Music, with an Accompaniment" (46-48). And the fleur-de-lis devices on Elizabeth's tomb as symbols of Elizabeth are treated below under *The Ring and the Book* (I.1-4, 15-17). In addition, there are three lyres engraved on the tomb of Elizabeth; the meaning of the lyres is discussed above under "Eurydice to Orpheus" (1-8).

PARLEYING WITH CHARLES AVISON

8:232-34, 248

Still on the Painter's fresco, from the hand
Of God takes Eve the life-spark whereunto
She trembles up from nothingness.
. . .
. . . Thanks. . . Angelo!

DeVane identifies this passage as a reference to Michelangelo's "fresco" of the Creation of "Eve," in the Sistine Chapel of the Vatican (DEVAN, 204, note). Another reference to the same fresco surfaces in "Parleying with Francis Furini" (*Comp.*, 221, 223, Fig. 120). And in this appendix above under the "Furini" poem (3:152-60), a composite allusion groups together Michelangelo's fresco *Creation of Eve*, Pen Browning's statue *Eve after Temptation*, and Francesco Furini's painting *Adam and Eve in Earthly Paradise*.

PAULINE

656-67 (cont. from *Comp.*, 224-27)

> Andromeda!
> And she is with me: years roll, I shall change,
> But change can touch her not—so beautiful
> With her fixed eyes, earnest and still, and hair
> Lifted and spread by the salt-sweeping breeze,
> And one red beam, all the storm leaves in heaven,
> Resting upon her eyes and hair, such hair,
> As she awaits the snake on the wet beach
> By the dark rock and the white wave just breaking
> At her feet; quite naked and alone; a thing
> I doubt not, nor fear for, secure some god
> To save will come in thunder from the stars.

A close examination of the two pictures of Perseus and Andromeda that are shown in the *Compendium* reveals that both versions are described, in part, in the present text (*Comp.*, 225, 226, Figs. 121, 122). The Andromeda by Volpato is partly clothed; whereas in the picture by Polidoro da Caravaggio she is indeed, as the text indicates, "quite naked." In the Volpato the "dark rock and the white wave just breaking / At her feet" are prominent, but in the version by Polidoro da Caravaggio the breaking wave is less pronounced and the rock is not dark.

The description of a breaking wave and a dark rock in this passage apparently furthers the discussion in the *Compendium* (224-27) establishing the Volpato as the version of Perseus and Andromeda that Browning had with him, that is, had hanging over his desk ("Andromeda! / And she is with me"). But the depiction here of a totally naked Andromeda also indicates that Browning either had seen or had in his possession a reproduction of the Polidoro da Caravaggio prior to the publication of *Pauline* in 1833. And this, surprisingly, was at least eleven years before he could have seen the original in Rome in 1844. Thus I enter the two pictures under this citation in the Summary of Composite Sources below and leave unresolved which version, if not both, Browning had mounted over his desk.

Other comparisons of the uses of different elements in the two pictures appear above under *Fifine at the Fair* (sections 47 and 49) and below under *The Ring and the Book* (VI.1987-96, VII.390-93, and IX.965-70).

PIETRO OF ABANO

55:436-38

> [Tiberius,] "Fling at Abano
> Golden dice," it [the Oracle] answered: "dropt within
> the fount there,
> Note what sum the pips present!"

All that remains of the "fount" or *Fountain of Tiberius*, as I have observed, is a circular bed of gravel about eight feet in diameter in the Archeological Zone of "Abano," Italy.

PIPPA PASSES

II.49-51 (cont. from *Comp.*, 241)

> . . . better that will look
> When cast in bronze—an Almaign Kaiser, that,
> Swart-green and gold, with truncheon based on hip.

Two "bronze" statues in the Court Church of Innsbruck, I propose, neatly fit Browning's text. One statue is an "Almaign Kaiser," or German emperor, and one is a German *König*, or king. Each has a "truncheon based on hip," that is, as I define it, a scepter held upright at the base at the level of the hip. One of the statues portrays König or King Albrecht I (1248-1308); it was designed by Hans Polhaimer, modelled by Leonhard Magt, and cast by Stefan Godl in 1527 (EGG, 16-17, Fig. 292). The other statue depicts Kaiser or Emperor Friedrich III (1415-1493); it was designed by Jörg Kölderer after Gilg Sesselschreiber in 1515, modelled by Leonhard Magt, and cast by Stefan Godl in 1522 (EGG, 10-11, Fig. 293). The description of the colors "Swart-green and gold" probably derives from the fact that bronze looks like gold when polished and turns green when tarnished. In Figure 293 the knob of the bottom of the scepter that Kaiser Friedrich holds is shiny like gold—no doubt from much handling by tourists—while the emperor's attire is considerably tarnished green from lack of cleaning. None of the other bronze statues in the Court Church so closely corresponds with Browning's text. Browning unquestionably saw the Court Church of Innsbruck, a popular tourist attraction, while passing through Innsbruck in 1838, three years prior to the publishing of *Pippa Passes*.

The "Swart-green and gold" colors of bronze signal the ensuing happy ending to the seemingly disastrous marriage between Jules and Phene: figuratively, Jules perceives beneath the dark green tarnish covering the surface of Phene's victimized life as a prostitute the gold-like value of her true character.

For the relationship of the bronze statues of Albrecht I and Friedrich III to the imaginary Neptune statue in "My Last Duchess," see above under that poem, lines 48-56, paragraph one.

PORPHYRIA'S LOVER

38-41

> . . . all her hair
> In one long yellow string I wound
> Three times her little throat around,
> And strangled her.

From biographical evidence, Woolford and Karlin suggest that a painting of Mary Magdalen by Titian provides the model for Porphyria's "yellow" hair (WOO, I, 330, note for lines 18-20), but they do not specify which of Titian's paintings of the subject is applicable.   Browning no doubt viewed the version in the Hermitage during his trip to Russia in 1834; yet the version in the Pitti Palace (Map F:9G), not seen in person by Browning before the publication of "Porphyria's Lover" in 1836, though possibly observed by him in reproduction, better displays golden hair around the "throat."   Consequently, since a case can be made for both paintings, I consider the two versions composite. (Figure 73, on page 147 in the *Compendium*, illustrates the *Magdalen* in the Pitti Palace, *not* the one in the Hermitage, as erroneously indicated on page 146.)

Above under "Cenciaja," lines 15-29, the art of Titian is considered sensual; here, as applied to the character of Porphyria, the sensuality of Titian's work is no less apt.

Another identification of a Mary Magdalen by Titian is made in the *Compendium* under "In a Gondola" (146, 147).

PRINCE HOHENSTIEL-SCHWANGAU, SAVIOUR OF SOCIETY

The end of the introduction to this poem in the Riverside
Edition of Browning's poems reads (BRO, 682):

> There is a palace Hohen-Schwangau, built by the Bavarian
> mad king Ludwig.

Figure 294 illustrates the palace or castle Hohen-Schwangau, the
famous tourist attraction, which is close by the more popular
Neuschwangau Castle, in the Bavarian Alps. The Riverside edi-
torial remark, as I read the association with the "Bavarian mad
king Ludwig" II, is a satire directed against Napoleon III, the
known model for Browning's Prince. Allan Dooley points out
that "Hohenstiel" means "*hohen-stile*" or "high-style" and that
Napoleon III had a German education and a predilection all his
life for German writers (DOO, 3, note to the title). Perhaps there
is satire further intended in the Prince's name in that a high
style, a German education, and a taste for German literature did
little to give Napoleon III the military skill to defeat Bismarck in
the Franco-Prussian War.

Another satirical image of Napoleon III in the poem under discussion crops up in the *Compendium* (247-48, 250, Fig.
135).

1986-97

> The little wayside temple, half-way down
> To a mild river. . .
>
> . . .
>
> I view that sweet small shrub-embedded shrine
> On the declivity, was sacred once
>
> . . .
>
> Well, how was it the due succession fell
> From priest to priest who ministered i' the cool
> Calm fane o'the Clitumnian god?

Figure 295 shows the "little wayside temple," the Temple of Clitumnus, a Christian building dating from the fifth century
(MI, 184). Browning, at the end of his poem, corrects the error
that this is the temple where priests systematically murdered
one another as a means to succession.

> . . . "Clitumnus" did I say?
> As if it had been his ox-whitening wave
> Whereby folk practised that grim cult of old—
> The murder of their temple's priest by who
> Would qualify for his succession. Sure—
> Nemi was the true lake's style. Dream had need
> Of the ox-whitening peace of prettiness
> And so confused names, well known once awake.

The correct place for "that grim cult of. . . succession," Browning leads us to believe, was presumably the Temple of Diana, by Lake "Nemi," in the Castelli Romani. Observation reveals that the ruins of the Temple of Diana are still visible at the foot of Lake Nemi just off Via del Tempio Diana, the road that leads down from the town of Nemi to the lake. A model of the temple is housed in the Museo delle Navi Romane, which is close to the ruins.

Allan Dooley gives the various legends behind Browning's account of succession by murder in the ancient Italian priesthood and explains that the point of Prince Hohenstiel's discourse is to show that "change from generation to generation cannot be controlled or predicted" (DOO, 101, note; also see PET, I, p. 1183, n. 1986, n. 2002-2007, and p. 1184, n. 2141).

PROTUS

52-57 (cont. from *Comp.*, 250, 251, 252)

> ["]A Protus of the race
> Is rumored to have died a monk in Thrace,—
> And if the same, he reached senility."
>
> Here's John the Smith's rough-hammered head. Great eye,
> Gross jaw and griped lips do what granite can
> To give you the crown-grasper. What a man!

The colossal bust of Constantine the Great is given as a possible source for this poem in the *Compendium* (252, Fig. 136). Symbolically, as the model for the imaginary Roman emperor "John the Smith," the bust underscores various Christian elements in the poem. Constantine the Great, we know, was the first Roman emperor to make Christianity a state religion, and he moved the capital at Rome to Byzantium and changed the name of the capital to New Rome and then to Constantinople. In Browning's poem, the imaginary emperor "Protus," who "Is rumored to have died a monk in Thrace," is clearly a Christian figure. The usurper "John the Pannonian" (line 36), who "Came, had a mind to take the crown" from Protus (line 39), was evidently a Christian in name, for presumably he lived when Protus was "Born in the porphyry chamber at Byzant" (line 10), when Byzantium had become Christian with the rule of Constantine the Great. And then "John let Protus live / And slip away" (lines 45-46), which indicates that John the Pannonian, to some degree, was also a Christian in charitable deed.

Also, see above under "Cleon," lines 82, 88-94, and compare the Christian theme in relation to the imaginary philosopher Cleon and the imaginary King Protus in that poem. The huge bust of Constantine the Great is further treated above under *Christmas-Eve and Easter-Day* (Pt. I, 12:749-52, 764-68); in that poem, the concern is with a criticism of Roman Catholicism.

THE RING AND THE BOOK

I.1-4, 15-17 (cont. from *Comp.*, 254-57, 439-41)

> Do you see this Ring?
>   'T is Rome-work, made to match
> (By Castellani's imitative craft)
> Etrurian circlets found. . .
>   . . .
> . . . hammer needs must widen out the round,
> And file emboss it fine with lily-flowers,
> Ere the stuff grow a ring-thing right to wear.

Dr. Giovanni Scichilone, Director of the National Museum of Villa Giulia, in Rome, called to my attention the inscription in Latin on the Castellani fleur-de-lis ring. The inscription reads, "*IN TE DOMINO CONFIDO*," "IN YOU GOD I TRUST," with the first letter of the inscription, "*I*," beginning at eleven-o'clock high on the face of the ring (*Comp.*, 415, Fig. 258). The inscription appears to be in relief, and this perhaps accounts for Browning's use of the word "emboss" in the text. But since the "lily-flowers" rather than the inscription should be embossed, a discrepancy arises that needs clarification.

Browning, we remember, visited the Castellani shop in 1860, eight years prior to publishing *The Ring and the Book*. (Figure 261 is a reproduction of the signatures of the Brownings

from the Castellani Guest-books; it was kindly provided by Dr.
Scichilone.) During that interim of eight years Browning could
have confused the lily design on the Castellani fleur-de-lis ring
with the fleur-de-lis devices he saw embossed on Medici coats of
arms in Florence. A good example of the latter is visible in Figure 257 (*Comp.*, 414; Map F:7H), which shows in relief a sculptured fleur-de-lis on the upper ball of the Medici coat of arms on
the pedestal for the statue of John of the Black Bands (see the
next entry). Also, there is an embossed fleur-de-lis device on the
upper ball of the Medici coat of arms over the arcade of the
courtyard in Palazzo Medici-Riccardi (*Comp.*, 441; Map F:7H). If,
then, the question in the text of the word "emboss" is clarified in
relation to the word "lily-flowers," it remains to make a connection between the religious Latin inscription in relief, "*IN TE
DOMINO CONFIDO*," IN YOU GOD I TRUST, and what
Browning leads us to believe is the embossed lily or fleur-de-lis
on the Castellani fleur-de-lis ring. I shall now demonstrate this
connection, which additionally involves four paintings and
sculptural elements on the tomb of Elizabeth Barrett Browning.

In religious symbolism, the fleur-de-lis stands for the Holy
Trinity—as indicated by the three petals of the device—and it
also represents the Holy Virgin; in art objects depicting the
Annunciation the lily is usually included as part of the subject
(WEB, 176-78). In *The Ring and the Book* Pompilia is many
times associated with the lily and the Virgin Mary (KING, VII,
p. 294, n. 687, p. 302, n. 58-59; ALT, p. 232, n. 4). Through the
conflation of two paintings implied in Book IV, lines 320-25, the
lily and the Virgin, as we shall see further on in this note, are
also types for Elizabeth Barrett Browning:

> . . . one child [Pompilia],
> The strange tall pale beautiful creature grown
> Lily-like out o' the cleft i' the sun-smit rock [in order]
> To bow its white miraculous birth of buds
> I' the way of wandering Joseph and his spouse,—
> So painters fancy. . . .

The two paintings are Gaudenzio Ferrari's *Flight into
Egypt* (Fig. 298) and Leonardo da Vinci's *Madonna of the Rocks*,
the version in the Louvre (*Comp.*, 417, Fig. 260); they are advanced as sources in the *Compendium*, pages 443-44 and 446-48.
In both paintings Pompilia is indirectly related to lilies. She is
typified in Leonardo's *Madonna of the Rocks* as a "pale beautiful

creature grown / Lily-like out o' the cleft i' the sun-smit rock,"
and in Ferrari's *Flight into Egypt* she is Joseph's "spouse," as one
of the same "Lily-like" flowers from Leonardo's painting is
placed in the Ferrari picture in order "To bow its white
miraculous birth of buds / I' the way of wandering Joseph and
his spouse,— / So painters fancy."

Congruent with Browning's imaginary transfer of a lily
from the Leonardo painting to the Ferrari painting is the historical influence of one painter on the other, for Ferrari was of the
Lombard tradition, which in turn owed much to Leonardo. In
particular, the facial contour, expression, and hair style of
Ferrari's Madonna and his use of a steep, rugged mountain in
the background of his painting owe something either to the
Madonna of the Rocks or to other paintings by Leonardo with
similar stylistic features (corroborated by EISE, in conversation,
August, 1993).

The transfer of biblical and stylistic elements from one
painting to the other, then, creates an imaginary conflation of
sources; the two discrepancies that occur in the process of the
conflation can be explained. The Leonardo *Madonna of the
Rocks* displays irises rather than lilies, but this divergence is ac-
counted for by the interchangeability of the iris with the lily in
Christian symbolism (*Comp.*, 443). The Ferrari *Flight into Egypt*,
instead of lilies, depicts fronds of a date tree that bend their fruit
to the Christ Child for nourishment (Fig. 298), but Browning
compensates for his insertion of a lily in lines 320-25 of Book IV,
as quoted above, by properly placing the date or "palm-tree"
within the context of lines 26-27 and 117-30 of Book IX:

> Suppose that Joseph, Mary and her Babe
> A-journeying to Egypt, prove the piece. . .
>
> . . . [by] the accomplished Ciro Ferri. . .
> . . .
> Thus then, just so and no whit otherwise,
> Have I,—engaged as I were Ciro's self,
> To paint a parallel, a Family,
> The patriarch Pietro with his wise old wife
> To boot (as if one introduced Saint Anne
> By bold conjecture to complete the group)
> And juvenile Pompilia with her babe,
> Who, seeking safety in the wilderness,
> Were all surprised by Herod, while outstretched
> In sleep beneath a palm-tree by a spring,
> And killed—the very circumstance I paint. . . .

This passage, like the one from Book IV, is an imaginary pictorial construct; it is modelled after the same *Flight into Egypt* by Ferrari and, instead of Leonardo's *Madonna of the Rocks*, two collateral paintings by Lodovico Mazzolino: his *Madonna with St. Anne* and his *Slaughter of the Innocents*, both of which are in the Uffizi Gallery. In the *Compendium*, pages 447-48, I justify this conflation of paintings through the correspondence of the text above with the subject matter of the paintings, the proximity of the paintings to each other in the Uffizi, Browning's acquaintance with the paintings, and the similarity between the name Ferrari and the name Ferri, the same "Ciro Ferri" who is given in the text here instead of Mazzolino. To this rationale I add the fact that Mazzolino came from the city of Ferrara, which further contributes to the case for a mistaken connection between the names of the painters Ferrari and Ferri. Finally, Browning could have confused Mazzolino's work with Ciro Ferri's because much of Ferri's painting is in the Palazzo Pitti (Map F:9G), which is near the Uffizi Gallery (Map F:8H).

For analysis, I shall now coordinate the four paintings just discussed with key words quoted from the citation out of Book IX given immediately above. Worked into the analysis is the symbolism of the Castellani fleur-de-lis ring and the tomb of Elizabeth Barrett Browning.

Elizabeth Barrett Browning shares the persona of the Holy Virgin with Pompilia in *The Ring and the Book* in three ways: 1) as an expansion of the Madonna typified as a lily and through the Flight-into-"Egypt" analogue in the combined Leonardo-Ferrari paintings; 2) as an extension of the Flight into Egypt and the Slaughter of the Holy "Family" with "Saint Anne" as conflated analogues in the Ferrari-Mazzolino paintings; and 3) through the symbolism of the inscription on the Castellani fleur-de-lis ring and the decorative motifs on the tomb of Elizabeth Barrett Browning. At the narrative level of meaning, Pompilia and Caponsacchi flee from Guido Franceschini, Pompilia's husband, just as "Mary" and "Joseph" escape from "Herod." "Pompilia" of course eventually fails in her efforts, and she and her parents ("Pietro" and his "wife," Violante, as "Saint Anne") are "killed" by Guido, as Herod. Mary's "Babe" in the analogue corresponds to Pompilia's "babe," Gaetano. At the biographical level, the Flight of the Holy Family becomes the elopement of the Brownings, with Elizabeth's father represented by Herod, and Pen, anachronistically, by the Christ Child; I say

anachronistically because Pen, of course, was born two and a half
years after the elopement of the Brownings.

The inscription on the Castellani fleur-de-lis ring, "*IN
TE DOMINO CONFIDO*," serves as a prayer for divine protection
for the eventual birth of Gaetano during the flight of Pompilia
and Caponsacchi; and, if one considers the delicate health of
Elizabeth, the inscription recalls the need for divine protection
during the elopement of the Brownings and protection for
Elizabeth's brothers and sisters from Mr. Barrett, who, though
obviously not as harsh as Herod, would have punished any
brother or sister whom he detected assisting the Brownings in
their elopement. ("*IN TE DOMINO CONFIDO*" means literally
"IN YOU GOD I CONFIDE"; Confidence is given above under
"Cleon," lines 82, 88-94, paragraph three, as one of the Christian
Virtues in George Herbert's poem "The Church Floor.")

The psychological basis for the idealization of Elizabeth
Barrett Browning as the Madonna is explained by Judith Bogert
in her article "The New Cross Knight: The Fixing of a Myth."
Idealization is a normal phase after a period of grief for coping
with the loss of a loved one; *The Ring and the Book*, having
been written shortly after the death of Elizabeth, served this purpose of helping Browning to withstand his loss (BOG, 35-36).
The idealization of Pen as the Christ Child indicates Browning's
hope in the future for a perpetuation, through his son, of the
memory of Elizabeth.

The fleur-de-lis device on the Castellani fleur-de-lis ring
as the emblem of the Holy Virgin, ergo Pompilia, ergo Elizabeth
Barrett Browning, is underscored by the large stylized fleur-de-lis
devices carved singly on each of the long sides of Elizabeth's
tomb. Also, on the frieze under the lid of the tomb are alternating embossed fleur-de-lis and daisy designs (*Comp.*, 88, Fig. 37;
ORMO, Fig. 100). Although Robert never saw Elizabeth's tomb
in person, he had at least one photograph of her tomb that he
was no doubt familiar with while he was writing *The Ring and
the Book* (KEL, 491, item H255; MER, p. 51, Plate 25, p. 84, item
56). Another possibility is the photograph that Browning had
hanging over his desk in De Vere Garden (KEL, 491, item, H253).
The photographs are further discussed above under "Parleying
with Gerard de Lairesse" (16:426-34).

Evidence that the daisy is also a symbol for Elizabeth
Barrett Browning is manifest above under "Flute-Music, with
an Accompaniment" (46-48) and "Parleying with Gerard de
Lairesse" (16:426-34).

I.38, 45-49 (cont. from *Comp.*, 257-60, 441-442)

I found this book,

. . .

Toward Baccio's marble,—ay, the basement-ledge
O' the pedestal where sits and menaces
John of the Black Bands with the upright spear,
'Twixt palace and church,—Riccardi where they lived,
His race, and San Lorenzo where they lie.

Compare the heart-shaped design for the Medici coats of arms on the pavement of the Medici Chapel, in the Church of "San Lorenzo," in Florence (Fig. 296; Map F:7H), with the heart-shaped design of the diamond betrothal ring of the Brownings (*Comp.*, 409, Fig. 252). Note that the coat of arms illustrated in Figure 296 has a fleur-de-lis device on the ball at the top of the design, which is true of all four Medici coats of arms on the pavement of the Medici Chapel. Recall that the fleur-de-lis device in *pietra dura* in the Medici Chapel is surmounted with a crown (*Comp.*, 410, Fig. 253; Map F:7H) and that the diamond betrothal ring of the Brownings is also capped by a crown (*Comp.*, 409, Fig. 252). And consider that there are large and small fleur-de-lis designs on the tomb of Elizabeth Barrett Browning (see the penultimate paragraph of the preceding entry, and the *Comp.*, 88, Fig. 37). The heart-shaped designs and the fleur-de-lis devices on the Medici coats of arms on the floor of the Medici Chapel and the fleur-de-lis designs on the tomb of Elizabeth Barrett Browning add further support to my hypothesis, with the assistance of Professor Eisenberg, that there is an emblematic connection between the diamond betrothal ring of the Brownings and the Medici family, that there is a particular association between the diamond betrothal ring and one of the Medici princes, Lorenzo the Magnificent, whose device was a diamond ring, that the link between Lorenzo and his patron saint, "San Lorenzo," should not go unnoticed, and that Browning, as a result of these connections, associated himself with Lorenzo the Magnificent as a poet and patron of art.

Examples of Browning acting as a patron or champion for the art of his son, Pen, emerge above under "Parleying with Francis Furini" (3:152-60, 11:601-07). Furini, it should be noted, rendered paintings about Lorenzo the Magnificent for the Pitti Palace, and maybe Furini's paintings about Lorenzo were images in Browning's mind while he was championing the art of his

son in the "Furini" poem. Certainly the connection is strengthened by Browning's use of another Furini painting in the Pitti
Palace, his *Adam and Eve in Earthly Paradise*, which, appropriately enough, is mentioned in the "Furini" poem (2:76-96, 3:152-
60).

Browning, as I indicate here and in the *Compendium*
(442), was also interested in Lorenzo the Magnificent as a poet.
Evidence of this interest goes back to an early translation of 1846,
in which Browning puts into English a quatrain in Italian by
Lorenzo (see WOO, II, 373).

> **I.1391-94, 1397-98** (cont. from *Comp.*, 281, 282, 416, 442-43)
>
> > O lyric Love, half angel and half bird,
> > And all a wonder and a wild desire,—
> > Boldest of hearts that ever braved the sun,
> > Took sanctuary within the holier blue,
> > . . .
> > When the first summons from the darkling earth
> > Reached thee amid thy chambers, blanched their blue. . . .

The word "holier" in the text "Took sanctuary within the holier
blue. . . amid thy chambers. . . blue" is the key to comparing
Elizabeth Barrett Browning's blue chambers, presumably in
heaven, with the light-blue ceiling of the master bedroom in
Casa Guidi. Unfortunately, Figure 259 was photographed before
the master bedroom was restored to its present color (*Comp.*, 416;
Map F:9G), and so the reader will have to use his imagination in
picturing the light-blue ceiling.

The two doves in relief on the ceiling of the master bedroom in Casa Guidi and Aert de Gelder's painting *Jacob's Dream*
are submitted in the *Compendium* as composite sources for the
image of Elizabeth as "half angel and half bird" (*Comp.*, pp. 281,
282, Fig. 157, p. 416, Fig. 259, pp. 442-43). Another possible allusion to Gelder's painting is discussed above under *Fifine at the
Fair* (123:2109-12).

> **VI.400-06, 667-73, 913-14** (revised and cont. from *Comp.*, 304, 305-06)
>
> > It was as when, in our cathedral once,
> > As I got yawningly through matin-song,
> > I saw *facchini* bear a burden up,

Base it on the high-altar, break away
A board or two, and leave the thing inside
Lofty and lone: and lo, when next I looked,
There was the Rafael!

Learned Sir,
I told you there's a picture in our church.
. . .
. . . "See a thing that Rafael made—
This venom issued from Madonna's mouth!"

. . .
Pictured Madonna raised her painted hand,
Fixed the face Rafael bent above the Babe. . . .

These three separate yet integrated texts in Book VI describe an imaginary painting by "Rafael" of a "Madonna" and "Babe" presumably over the high altar of the "cathedral" or Duomo of Arezzo. My choice of a source for the imaginary painting is the marble relief of the Madonna and Child that is actually over the high altar of the Duomo of Arezzo. The relief is part of the monument for St. Donatus, and it was probably rendered in the thirteenth century by Betto di Francesco and Giovanni di Francesco. This identification, which I give in the *Compendium* (304, 305-06), explains Browning's placement of a Madonna and Child in the Cathedral of Arezzo; it does not account for the attribution of the Madonna and Child in the text to Raphael. In light of this problem, Marvin Eisenberg advances Raphael's *Small Cowper Madonna* as a possible collateral source, and I add to the conflation by nominating Raphael's *Madonna del Granduca*. The reasoning behind these proposals follows a circularity of associations among the sources advanced. The Madonna and Child on the monument for St. Donatus resembles Raphael's *Small Cowper Madonna* because the Christ Child in both representations is what art historians call "lively" (*Comp.*, p. 381, Fig. 224, p. 385, Fig. 228). The *Small Cowper Madonna* is similar to the *Madonna del Granduca* in that there is a correspondence between the faces and in that the date given to the fashioning of these two paintings by Raphael is 1505. And the three-quarter frontal view of the *Madonna del Granduca* and the heavy folds of the garment on the Madonna's right side match the three-quarter frontal view and the heavy folds of the garment on the right side of the Madonna on the monument for St. Donatus (*Comp.*, p. 210, Fig. 111, p. 381, Fig. 224).

Also, the identifications of the *Madonna del Granduca* as a source in "One Word More" (*Comp.*, 206) and as a source for the Madonna in "Parleying with Christopher Smart," which is entered above under that poem, further emphasize the vividness of the *Madonna del Granduca* in Browning's mind.

New evidence of the correspondence between the *Small Cowper Madonna* and the *Madonna and Child* by Betto and Giovanni Francesco is that the somewhat level heads of the Madonna and Child in the *Small Cowper Madonna* form an upright triangle and that the fairly level heads of the Madonna and Child in the Francesco relief form an inverted triangle (*Comp.*, p. 381, Fig. 224, p. 385, Fig. 228). This, I admit, is a subtle relationship, but it should be mentioned since the *Small Cowper Madonna* is the only Madonna by Raphael, among the approximately fifty that he did, in which the head of the Christ Child is somewhat level with that of the Madonna (corroborated by EISE, August, 1993).

Finally, conclusive evidence that Browning conflated the work of Raphael with the relief on the monument for St. Donatus stands out in the third of the three citations from Book VI of *The Ring and the Book*, lines 913-14:

> Pictured Madonna raised her painted hand,
> Fixed the face Rafael bent above the Babe. . . .

Clearly, as is seen in Figure 224 (*Comp.*, 381), the so-called "painted hand"—the right hand—of the "Pictured Madonna" is "raised" (some fingers on the hand are missing), and her "face," presumably by "Rafael," is "bent above the Babe."

A discussion of the association of the Madonna and Child with Pompilia Franceschini and Elizabeth Barrett Browning is involved in the note above under this poem for Book I, lines 1-4, 15-17.

VI.1987-96

> Nor am I
> Infatuated,—oh, I saw, be sure!
> Her brow had not the right line, leaned too much,
> Painters would say; they like the straight-up Greek:
> This seemed bent somewhat with an invisible crown
> Of martyr and saint, not such as art approves.
> And how the dark orbs dwelt deep underneath,
> Looked out of such a sad sweet heaven on me!

> The lips, compressed a little, came forward too,
> Careful for a whole world of sin and pain.

What "Painters would say" if they knew the model that Browning had in mind for this description by Caponsacchi of the features of Pompilia's face is that it is an allusion to the versions of Andromeda by Volpato and Polidoro da Caravaggio. Painters would particularly say, as delineated in Figures 121 and 122 (*Comp.*, 225 and 226), that Pompilia's face, with the likeness of Andromeda's visage, did not have the ideal "straight-up Greek" profile; rather "Her brow. . . leaned too much. . . seemed bent somewhat with an invisible crown." Furthermore, her "dark orbs dwelt deep underneath," and her "lips, compressed a little, came forward too." This depiction could be said for both versions of Andromeda except that the lips in the Polidoro da Caravaggio are more open than compressed.

Other descriptions differentiating the various features of Andromeda in these two pictures are considered above under *Fifine at the Fair* (sections 47 and 49), *Pauline* (656-67), and below under this poem (VII.390-93 and IX.965-70).

VII.390-93 (cont. from *Comp.*, 315-16)

> . . .
> (Tisbe had told me that the slim young man
> With wings at head, and wings at feet, and sword
> Threatening a monster, in our tapestry,
> Would eat a girl else,—was a cavalier). . . .

Both the versions of Perseus and Andromeda by Polidoro da Caravaggio and Volpato are represented in this imaginary "tapestry." As Figures 121 and 122 illustrate (*Comp.*, 225, 226), Perseus enters the scene "With wings at head, and wings at feet, and sword / Threatening a monster." Other allusions that borrow different elements from the two pictures occur above under *Fifine at the Fair* (sections 47 and 49), *Pauline* (656-67), and under this poem (VI.1987-96 and IX.965-70).

In the *Ring and the Book*, there are two levels of meaning in established analysis of the characters in the Perseus and Andromeda myth and its Christian counterparts, the legends of St. George and the Dragon and of St. Michael and Satan. At the narrative level, St. George and St. Michael are Caponsacchi rescuing Pompilia from Guido Franceschini; biographically, level, the champion is Robert Browning eloping with Elizabeth in opposition to her father (DEVANE; KING, VII, 277).

References or allusions to the Perseus and Andromeda myth that are developed under this poem are listed in the first paragraph of this note. (Under Book IX, lines 965-70, the Andromeda myth is implied, while what is overtly described is the Hesione legend, which is a counterpart of the Andromeda myth.) References to the legends of St. George and the Dragon or St. Michael and Satan that are treated under this poem are entered in the *Compendium* under Book VII, lines 1215-19 (*Comp.*, 316-17, Fig. 179), Book VII, lines 1323-28 (*Comp.*, 318, Fig. 180), and Book X, lines 1010-12 (*Comp.*, 321, 322-23, Figs. 181, 182); in this appendix see below under Book X, lines 1010-12.

IX.803-06

> . . .　　　　　　　　[Pompilia]
> Hold[s], as it were, a deprecating hand,
> Statuesquely, in the Medicean mode,
> Before some shame which modesty would veil?
> Who blames the gesture prettily perverse?

Cook associates the phrase "Statuesquely, in the Medicean mode," with the *Medici Venus*, in the Uffizi Gallery (COOK, 190; Fig. 279; Map F:8H). Compare the entry under Book IX, lines 169-71, in the *Compendium*, page 320, as a possible antecedent for this text.

The statue expresses for Bottinius his ambivalent attitude toward Pompilia's innocence. The hands of Venus—as Pompilia's—either shield her nakedness, "which modesty would veil," or hide "some shame."

IX.965-70 (cont. from *Comp.*, 320-21)

> Methinks I view some ancient bas-relief.
> There stands Hesione thrust out by Troy,
> Her father's hand has chained her to a crag,
> Her mother's from the virgin plucked the vest,
> At a safe distance both distressful watch,
> While near and nearer comes the snorting orc.

In one way the identification in the *Compendium* (321) of "some ancient bas-relief" with Polidoro da Caravaggio's *Perseus and Andromeda* is correct. Andromeda's mother has "from the virgin plucked the vest" so that Andromeda is presumably naked, that is, naked if "vest" means vesture (*Comp.*, 225, Fig. 121); in the version by Volpato (*Comp.*, 226, Fig. 122) she is partly dressed.

In another particular, however, there is a correspondence between the two versions of the subject. The "mother" and "father" of Andromeda "At a safe distance both distressful watch" the plight of Andromeda as she is "chained. . . to a crag." Her parents ostensibly are not visible in Figure 121, the Polidoro version, but I assure the reader, having viewed the picture in the Museo di Roma (Map R:8G), that the father and the mother are to be seen in the upper left-hand part of the picture just as they appear in Figure 122, the Volpato version of the scene (also see AL, 37-38, Plates 6 and 7, taken from MA, II, 136-37).

Differences between other descriptions of the two pictures are noted above under *Fifine at the Fair* (sections 47 and 49), *Pauline* (656-67), and under the present poem (VI.1987-96 and VII.390-93).

Bottinius, in his prosecution of Guido Franceschini, gives one analogue and implies another in this passage. Pompilia is both "Hesione" and Andromeda; Pompilia's "mother," Violante, and her "father," Pietro, are Cassiopeia and Cepheus in the Andromeda myth; Pompilia's father is King Laomedon of "Troy" in the Hesione legend, whose "hand has chained her [Hesione] to a crag"; Pompilia's husband, Guido, is the dragon or "snorting orc" of the two stories. Pompilia's champion, Caponsacchi, the reader is left to presume, is either Perseus, who saves Andromeda, or Hercules, who rescues Hesione.

X.233-35

> Therefore there is not any doubt to clear
> When I shall write the brief word presently
> And chink the hand-bell, which I pause to do.

Cook identifies the "hand-bell" in this passage and in lines 203 and 282 of Book X as the silver hand-bell which lies upright on the table in Raphael's portrait of Pope Leo X, in the Uffizi (COOK, 206; Fig. 262; Map F:8H; at one time the painting was housed in the Pitti Palace). Note the other allusion to Raphael's painting (*Comp.*, 420), the allusion to Andrea del Sarto's copy of Raphael's painting (*Comp.*, 28), and Figure 263 in this appendix.

X.1010-12 (cont. from *Comp.*, 266, 321, 322-23)

Armed and crowned,

Would Michael, yonder, be, nor crowned nor armed,
The less pre-eminent angel?

Compare the marble statue of St. Michael by Raffaello da Montelupo with the bronze one by Verschaffelt (*Comp.*, p. 322,
Fig. 181, p. 323, Fig. 182; Map R:6F,7F). Characteristically, both
statues are "armed" with swords, but only the one by Raffaello
da Montelupo is "crowned." The shape of the crown is not fully
visible in Figure 181; however, the form of the crown, as seen
from above the statue, is clearly that of a headband. This description corrects Cook and King, who erroneously place the crown
on the head of the *Michael* by Verschaffelt (COOK, 215; KING, IX,
317). Historically, too, the statue by Raffaello da Montelupo
coincides with Browning's text. Pope Innocent XII, before the
execution of Guido Franceschini in 1698, could only have seen
Raffaello's "Michael, yonder," yonder from the Vatican, that is,
surmounting Castel Sant'Angelo, for not until 1753 was the
Verschaffelt replacement hoisted to the top of the castle. The
proper source for Browning's text, therefore, is the Raffaello da
Montelupo, while the Verschaffelt is discredited.

The symbolism of the legend of St. Michael and Satan
through art in this poem, along with the counterpart legend of
St. George and the Dragon, is treated above under Book VII, lines
390-93.

XI.184-88 (cont. from *Comp.*, 325-26, 327-28)

. . .

[I] Came on your fine axe in a frame, that falls
And so cuts off a man's head underneath,
Mannaia,—thus we made acquaintance first:
Out of the way, in a by-part o' the town,
At the Mouth-of-Truth o' the river-side, you know. . . .

Roma King points out that the "Mouth-of-Truth," the mascaron,
or mask of a Triton in the shape of a disc, stands for Guido's
head and that Guido foreshadows his execution by "Mannaia"—
by guillotine (KING, IX, 331; *Comp.*, 327-28, Figs. 185, 186). Another omen of death for Guido is represented in Book II, lines
83-96, through reference to Guido Reni's painting of the Crucifixion in the Church of San Lorenzo in Lucina (*Comp.*, 281, 283,

284, Fig. 158; Map R:6H).

Art is also employed throughout *The Ring and the Book* as portents of death for the Comparini family. These portents are the burial grounds of the Capuchin Church in Rome, whose walls are decorated with the bones of monks (Book I.896-903: *Comp.*, pp. 274, 276, Fig. 153; Map R:6I); Pietro Bernini's fountain in Piazza di Spagna, which is in the shape of a boat that appears to be sinking (Book III.388-93: *Comp.*, pp. 287, 288-289, Fig. 161; Map R:6I); the malignant lion statue of the Church of San Lorenzo in Lucina (Book VII.21-27: *Comp.*, pp. 311, 313, Fig. 177; Map R:6H); descriptions of a monster in a tapestry and on a bas-relief attacking Andromeda and/or Hesione (Books VII.390-93, IX.965-70: *Comp.*, p. 225, Fig. 121, p. 226, Fig. 122, pp. 315-16, 320-21, *App. A*, same citations); and the bronze sculpture of the three-headed monster Chimaera (Book XI.1115-25: *Comp.*, pp. 329-30, Fig. 188).

SORDELLO

III.136-37, 876-77 (cont. from *Comp.*, 349, 350, 351, 353)

> . . .
> What pillar, marble massive, sardius slim,
> 'T were fittest he transport to Venice' Square. . . .
>
> . . . prisoned in the Piombi, I repeat
> Events one rove occasioned, o'er and o'er. . . .

The possible influence on these passages of Lord Byron's *Childe Harold's Pilgrimage*, Canto IV, is noted below under "A Toccata of Galuppi's," lines 5-8.

A SOUL'S TRAGEDY (cont. from *Comp.*, 362, 364)

Act. II [Stage directions]

> *The Market-place.* LUITOLFO *in disguise mingling with the* Populace *assembled opposite the* Provost's *Palace.*

Some readers might have difficulty visualizing how the description in the *Compendium* (364) of the Provost's Palace of Faenza is, as I put it, "surrounded by an arcade surmounted by a gallery, which was obviously added at a later time." As Figure 212 illustrates, the medieval castellation of the Provost's Palace is in stylistic contrast with the Renaissance columns of the arcade and gallery, and the three round arches of the windows to the Palace are seen to be almost completely blocked off by the addition of the arcade and gallery.

A TOCCATA OF GALUPPI'S

5-8 (cont. from *Comp.*, 369-71)

> What, they lived once thus at Venice where
>   the merchants were the kings,
> Where St.Mark's is, where the Doges used
>   to wed the sea with rings?
>
> Ay, because the sea's the street there; and
>   't is arched by. . . what you call
> . . . Shylock's bridge with houses on it, where
>   they kept the carnival. . . .

Compare this citation with Lord Byron's *Childe Harold's Pilgrimage*, Canto IV, stanza 4, lines 4-6, which Stefan Hawlin implies but does not specify as a source (HAWL, 498):

>   . . .
> Above the dogeless city's vanished sway:
> Ours is a trophy which will not decay
> With the Rialto; Shylock and the Moor. . . .

In 1797 the eleven-hundred-year line of the doges was brought to an end, and the "dogeless city," with its "Rialto" or "Shylock's bridge" (*Comp.*, 371, Fig. 217), was occupied by the French. Prior to this date the "Doges used to wed the sea with rings" on his golden barge, the *Bucentaur*, every year on Ascension day. Figure 299 displays a model of the *Bucentaur*, which is housed in the Naval Museum of Venice. The original ship was burned by the French. (Compare with the discussion above under "My Last Duchess," lines 48-56, paragraph four.)

Also mentioned in *Childe Harold's Pilgrimage* are the "Bridge of Sighs" (Canto IV, stanza 1, line 1) and the "wingéd lion's marble piles" (IV,1:8). Corresponding references to these landmarks in Venice are described under *Sordello*, Part III, lines

136-37 and 876-77 (*Comp.*, p. 349, Fig. 201, right pillar, pp. 350, 351, 353, Fig. 204; see above under Sor, same citations).

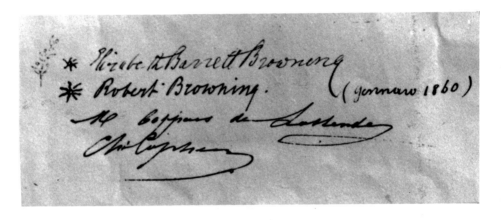

Fig. 261
Signatures of the Brownings (actual size)
Castellani Guest-books
January ("gennaio"), 1860
National Museum of Villa Giulia
Rome

Fig. 262
Raphael
Pope Leo X with Two Cardinals
Uffizi
Florence

Fig. 263
Andrea del Sarto
Pope Leo X with Two Cardinals, after Raphael
Museo di Capodimonte
Naples

Fig. 264
Andrea del Sarto
Madonna of the Harpies
Uffizi
Florence

Fig. 265
Raphael
Madonna of the Goldfinch
Uffizi
Florence

Fig. 266
Leonardo da Vinci
Adoration of the Magi
Uffizi
Florence

Fig. 267
Michelangelo
Doni Holy Family
Uffizi
Florence

Fig. 268
Villa Medicea
Poggio a Caiano
(environs of Florence)

Fig. 269
Andrea del Sarto
Caesar Presented with Tribute
Sala Grande, Villa Medicea
Poggio a Caiano
(environs of Florence)

Fig. 270
Alesso Baldovinetti
Nativity (detail)
Cloister of the Madonna
Church of the Santissima Annunziata
Florence

Fig. 271
Andrea del Sarto
Birth of the Virgin (detail)
Cloister of the Madonna
Church of the Santissima Annunziata
Florence

Fig. 272
Chapel of St. Ignatius Loyola
Church of the Gesù
Rome

Fig. 273
Globe of lapis lazuli
Chapel of St. Ignatius Loyola
Church of the Gesù
Rome

Fig. 274
William Etty
The Sirens and Ulysses
Manchester City Art Gallery
Manchester
England

Fig. 275
Sir Joshua Reynolds
Garrick between Tragedy and Comedy, about 1761
(private collection)

Fig. 276
Georg Mayr and Joachim Pais
Fountain of Neptune
Piazza delle Erbe
Bolzano
Italy

Fig. 277
Gerard de Lairesse
Zeus
from *The Art of Painting*

Fig. 278
Apollo Belvedere
Museo Pio-Clementino
Vatican

Fig. 279
Medici Venus
Uffizi
Florence

Fig. 280
Domenico Ghirlandaio
St. Jerome in His Study
Church of Ognissanti
Florence

Fig. 281
Botticelli
St. Augustine in His Study
Church of Ognissanti
Florence

Fig. 282
Giovanni Toscani
The Penitent St. Jerome
Princeton University Art Museum
Princeton, New Jersey

Fig. 283
Lorenzo Monaco
San Benedetto Altarpiece
(with detail)
National Gallery
London

Fig. 284
Francesco Furini
Venus Mourning the Death of Adonis
Academy of Fine Arts
Budapest

Fig. 285
Francesco Furini
Adam and Eve in Earthly Paradise
Pitti Palace
Florence

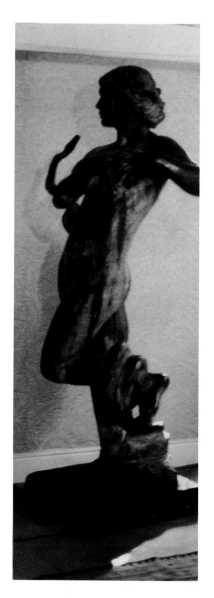

Fig. 286
Pen Browning
Dryope

Left: Armstrong Browning Library
               (from a photograph)
               Waco, Texas
Right: Private collection
               England

Fig. 287
Pen Browning
Joan of Arc and the Kingfisher
Trask Family Estate
(Yaddo Foundation)
Saratoga Springs, New York

Fig. 288
Pen Browning
Still Life of Fruits and Vegetables
Clapp Library, Special Collections
Wellesley College
Wellesley, Massachusetts

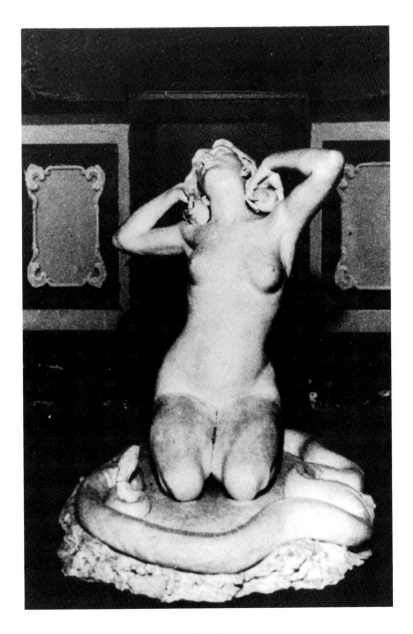

Fig. 289
Pen Browning
Eve after Temptation
(from a photograph)
Armstrong Browning Library
Waco, Texas

Fig. 290
Gerard de Lairesse
Fable of Dryope (detail)
from *The Art of Painting*

Fig. 291
Gerard de Lairesse
Venus Mourning Adonis
from *The Art of Painting*

Fig. 293
Gilg Sesselschreiber, Jörg Kölderer,
Leonhard Magt, and Stefan Godl
Kaiser Friedrich III
Court Church
Innsbruck

Fig. 294
Hohen-Schwangau Castle
Füssen, Bavaria
Germany

Fig. 295
Temple of Clitumnus
Spoleto (environs)
Italy

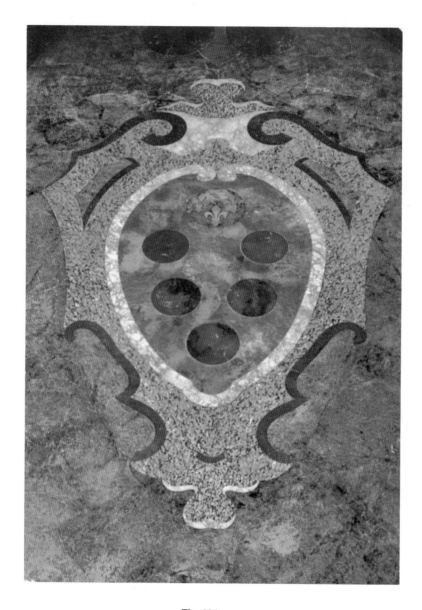

Fig. 296
Medici Coat of Arms
Cappella de'Principi
Church of San Lorenzo
Florence

Fig. 297
Battle of Isso (with detail)
Archeological Museum
Naples

Fig. 298
Gaudenzio Ferrari
Flight into Egypt
Church of Santa Maria delle Grazie
Varallo
Italy

Fig. 299
Bucentaur (model)
Naval Museum
Venice

Fig. 300
Constantine the Great (detail)
Conservatori Museum
Rome

SUMMARY OF COMPOSITE SOURCES

The entries below supplement, revise, and correct the entries under the Summary of Composite Sources in the *Compendium*, pages 451-457. Definitions for sources that are termed "real," "unspecified," "imaginary," and "composite" are given in the Introduction of this appendix. Browning's creative method in formulating composites is reconsidered in the Introduction of this appendix and attributed variously to absentmindedness, an occasional faulty memory, and poetic license. Composites, both unspecified and imaginary, provide a basis for future research and add the element of diversity to my claim that Browning, in the above-mentioned Introduction, qualifies as the most pictorial ("painterly"), sculptural, and architectural of all poets.

Entries that are designated "(I)" are imaginary; those that are marked "(U)" are unspecified. Locations of the composite sources in this study are abbreviated as follows: *Comp.* = main body of citations and notes in the *Compendium*; Supp. = supplement to the main body of citations and notes in the *Compendium*; *App.* = *Appendix A*. The line numbers for each entry are not necessarily in exact correspondence between the *Compendium*; supplement to the *Compendium*, and *Appendix A*.

And, 103-12 (U) *(Comp., App.)*
Copy of a painting by Raphael: *Madonna of the Palazzo Tempi*, *Pope Leo X with Two Cardinals*, by Raphael; copy of Raphael's *Pope Leo X with Two Cardinals*, by Andrea del Sarto.

148-51 (U) (Supp.)
Work of Andrea del Sarto in France: *Portrait of the Infant Dauphin*; *Charity*.

259-63 (I) (*Comp.*, Supp., *App.*)
Four walls in the "New Jerusalem" painted by Andrea del Sarto, Raphael, Michelangelo, and Leonardo da Vinci: Cloister of the Madonna, Church of the Santissima Annunziata; Sala Grande, Villa Medicea, Poggio a Caiano; four paintings in the Uffizi Gallery; Life of Michelozzo, from Vasari's *Vite*; description of the "holy Jerusalem," in the Bible, Revelation 21:10-21.

Any, **77-78 (U)** (*Comp.*)
Painting of a reclining Venus by Titian: *Venus of Urbino*; *Venus and Cupid*; *Venus with the Organ-player*; *Venus with the Lute-player*; *Pardo Venus*.

Bi, **666-68 (U)** (Supp.)
Painting of St. Michael in repose: *St. Michael*, by Mabuse; *St. Michael*, by Innocenzo da Imola.

Bis, **56-61 (I)** (*Comp.*, Supp.)
Decorated tomb of a bishop in the Church of Santa Prassede: *Pan and Syrinx*, by Gerard Hoet; *Pan Pursuing Syrinx*, by Hendrick van Balen; *Pan and Syrinx*, by Hendrick Goltzius; *Pan and Syrinx*, by Rubens-Brueghel; tombs of Cardinal Cetti and Cardinal Anchero, in the Church of Santa Prassede.

By, **2:6-8 (U)** (*Comp.*)
Fireplaces: in the Dining Room and Drawing Room of Casa Guidi.

14:66-68, 18:86-90 (I) (*Comp.*, Supp., *App.*)
Chapel in the Alps with a fresco of John in the Desert on the façade: detail from the *Life of John the Baptist*, *Birth of John the Baptist*, by Filippo Lippi; Oratorio di Refubbri, near Bagni di Lucca; John Murray's *Handbook for Travellers in Switzerland, the Alps of Savoy and Piedmont*.

Cen, **15-29 (I)** (*Comp.*, *App.*)
Portrait of Beatrice Cenci by Titian: *Beatrice Cenci*, attributed to Guido Reni; Hilda's copy of Guido Reni's *Beatrice Cenci*, in Hawthorne's *The Marble Faun*.

Chr, **Pt.I,12:749-52, 764-68 (U)** *(Comp., App.)*
Statue of a colossus: "Ozymandias," by Shelley; *Constantine the Great*, the gigantic head and feet of the statue.

Cle, **82-94 (I)** *(Comp., App.)*
Checkered pavement of Cleon's courtyard: "The Church Floor," by George Herbert; decorated pavement in the Duomo of Siena.

Fif, **sections 47, 48, 49 (I)** *(App.)*
Triptych drawn in the sand and partly modelled after the style of Gérôme: *Perseus and Andromeda*, by Polidoro da Caravaggio; *Garrick between Comedy and Tragedy, about 1761)*, by Sir Joshua Reynolds; *Perseus and Andromeda*, by Volpato.

Fra, **70-75 (U)** *(Comp.)*
Picture of St. Jerome by or attributed to Filippo Lippi in the act of flagellation and/or related to the Medici family: *Four Fathers of the Church, Madonna with the Christ Child, Death of St. Jerome, Adoration of the Christ Child, Trinity and Saints, Suffering Christ between St. Francis and St. Jerome, Three Saints, St. Jerome*, by Filippo Lippi; *Penitent St. Jerome*, by Toscani; "Bishop Blougram's Apology," lines 704-07.

145-63 (U) *(Comp., Supp.)*
Figures representing monks of various shapes painted by Filippo Lippi: *Innovation of the Rule of the Carmelites*, by Filippo Lippi; *Consecration*; by Masaccio.

145-63 (U) *(Comp.)*
Picture of the Crucifixion by Filippo Lippi: *Trinity and Saints*, by Filippo Lippi; *Crucifixion and Saints* (2), one by Filippo Lippi and Pesellino, one by the school of Filippo Lippi.

145-63 (U) *(Comp.)*
Picture representing a girl on tiptoe by Filippo Lippi: *Madonna and Child and Life of St. Anne, Birth of St. Stephen*, by Filippo Lippi.

189-90 (U) (*Comp.*, Supp.)
Picture of a saint praising God by Giotto: *St. Francis Glorified in Heaven*, by the school of Giotto; *Life of St. Francis*, a fresco program attributed to Giotto, Church of San Francesco, Assisi.

265-69 (U) (*Comp.*)
Picture rendered in the early 1500's representing Eve: *The Temptation*, by Masolino; *The Expulsion*, by Masaccio; *Creation of Eve*, by Ghiberti; *Creation*, by Jacopo della Quercia; *Creation of Eve*, by Uccello.

286-90 (U) (*Comp.*, Supp.)
Florentine landscapes as backgrounds in fifteenth-century pictures: numerous landscapes for pictures by Filippo Lippi; *Tribute Money*, by Masaccio; *Alton Locke* and *Yeast*, by Charles Kingsley.

323-32 (I) (*Comp.*, Supp.)
Fresco of St. Lawrence by Filippo Lippi in Prato: *Martyrdom of St. Lawrence*, by Mario Balassi and Carlo Dolci; *Martyrdom of St. Lawrence*, by Fra Angelico; *Christ at the Column*, by Andrea del Castagno.

345-87 (I) (*Comp.*, Supp.)
A Coronation of the Virgin with a Christ Child and a St. Lucy by Filippo Lippi: *Coronation of the Virgin*, by Filippo Lippi; *Madonna and Child with Four Saints*, by Filippo Lippi; Legend of St. Lucy, from *Sacred and Legendary Art*, by Mrs. Anna Jameson.

Gra, **13-16, 31-34 (U)** (Supp., *App.*)
Setting for the poem: the Citadels of San Marino; Olympus, home of the Greek gods; "Empedocles on Etna," by Matthew Arnold.

In, **190-93 (U)** (*Comp.*, Supp.)
Painting of Mary Magdalen by Giorgione: *St. Mary Magdalen in Penitence* (2), by Titian; *Magdalen*, attributed to Giorgione.

Inap, 3-4, 12-14 (U) (*App.*)
Tower in Asolo, Italy: La Rocca (Castle of Asolo), Castle of
Catherine Cornaro.

Jam,   VIII.27-32 (I) (*Comp.*)
Literary clay cast of a hand with a ringed finger: *Clasped
Hands of the Brownings*, by Harriet Hosmer; *Loulie's
Hand*, by Hiram Powers; Kenyon's marble hand of Hilda,
in Hawthorne's *The Marble Faun*.

My,   1-4 (U) (*Comp.*)
Portrait of Lucrezia de'Medici: *Lucrezia de'Medici*, by Agnolo Bronzino and Alessandro Allori (5); medals nos. 473-
476 of Lucrezia de'Medici, by Pastorino da Siena; a bronze
medal of Lucrezia, by Francesco Salviati; a medal of Lucrezia, by Domenico Poggini; *A Young Lady*, from the Italian School in the Dulwich Picture Gallery; statue scene
from *The Winter's Tale*, by Shakespeare.

47-48 (I) (*Comp., App.*)
Setting for the poem: Ferrara, Este Castle; Venice, Ducal
Palace.

54-56 (I) (*Comp., App.*)
Neptune statue by Claus of Innsbruck: *Wonders of the Lit-
tle World*, by Wanley; fountain of Neptune in the Piazza
delle Erbe, Bolzano; bronze statues of Albrecht I and
Friederich III, in the Court Church of Innsbruck; statue of
Neptune in the Piazza della Borsa, Trieste; two statues of
Neptune in Venice, by Jacopo Sansovino; fountain group
sculpture of Neptune, by Giongo, in Trent; Neptune
chalice and Neptune vase, in the Residenz of Munich;
Venice Receives the Homage of Neptune, by Giambattista
Tiepolo.

Old,   13:97-104
Classical sculpture representing Alexander: *Dying
Alexander*, in the Uffizi Gallery; *Alexander Sarcophagus*,
in the Istanbul Museum **(U)** (*Comp.*).

Classical statue of Apollo: *Apollo Belvedere, Omphalos
Apollo* **(U)** (*Comp., App.*).

24:185-87 (U) (*Comp.*, Supp.)
Damaged frescoes in Florence: *Innovation of the Rule of the Carmelites*, by Filippo Lippi; *Portrait of Dante*, attributed to Giotto; *Last Supper*, by Ghirlandaio; *Lives of the Virgin and St. John the Baptist*, by Orcagna; *Christ at the Column*, by Andrea del Castagno; frescoes in the refectory of the Church of Santa Croce.

One, **2:5-17**
Paintings by Raphael representing his loved one: *La Velata*, *La Fornarina*, *Sistine Madonna*, Mary Magdalen in the *St. Cecilia*, *Portrait of a Lady* **(U)** (*Comp.*).

Sonnets written on sketches for the *Disputa* and *La Fornarina*, by Raphael **(U)** (*Comp.*, Supp.).

16:164 (U) (*Comp.*)
Towers used for Galileo's experiments: Galileo's Villa Gioiella, in Arcetri, near Florence; Bell-tower (Leaning Tower) of Pisa; Torre del Gallo, in Arcetri, near Florence.

Par, **3:152-60 (U)** (*Comp.*, *App.*)
Eve as the subject for an art object: *Creation of Eve*, by Michelangelo; *Adam and Eve in Earthly Paradise*, by Francesco Furini; *Eve after Temptation*, *Dryope* (bronze version), by Pen Browning.

Parl, **5:116-26 (U)** (*App.*)
Sculptures of Dryope and Eve by Pen Browning: *Eve after Temptation*; *Dryope*, one plaster and one bronze sculpture.

Pau, **656-67 (U)** (*Comp.*, *App.*)
Picture of Perseus and Andromeda: *Perseus and Andromeda*, by Polidoro da Caravaggio; *Perseus and Andromeda*, by Volpato.

Pic, **25-26, 31-33 (U)** (*Comp.*)
Painting of a Madonna carried in procession: *Rucellai Madonna*, by Duccio (Life of Cimabue, from Vasari's *Lives*); *Maestà*, by Duccio.

Pip, **II.49-51 (U)** (*Comp.*, *App.*)
Bronze statue of a German "Kaiser": bronze statues of König Albrecht I and Kaiser Friederich III, in the Hofkirche, Innsbruck.

III.162-63 (U) (*Comp.*)
Painting by Titian in Treviso: *Annunciation, Portrait of Speroni.*

Por, **38-41 (U)** (*App.*)
Model for Porphyria's golden hair: *St. Mary Magdalen in Penitence* (two versions), by Titian.

Rin, **I.1-4, 15-17 (I)** (*Comp.*, Supp., *App.*)
Etruscan style gold ring by Castellani with lily design: Robert Browning *Vis Mea* ring; Castellani fleur-de-lis ring; literary *Vis Mea* Etruscan ring in Isa Blagden's novel *Agnes Tremorne.*

I.1391-1401 (U) (*Comp.*, Supp., *App.*)
Image of Elizabeth Barrett Browning as a "lyric Love, half angel and half bird": *Jacob's Dream*, a painting by Aert de Gelder; doves in relief on the ceiling of the master bedroom in Casa Guidi.

IV.320-25 (I) (Supp., *App.*)
Painting of a Flight into Egypt with a bowing lily plant among rocks: *Madonna of the Rocks*, the version in the Louvre, by Leonardo da Vinci; *Flight into Egypt*, by Gaudenzio Ferrari.

VI.400-06 (I) (*Comp.*, *App.*)
Painting of a Madonna in Arezzo by Raphael: *Madonna and Child*, by Betto di Francesco and Giovanni di Francesco; *Small Cowper Madonna, Madonna del Granduca*, by Raphael.

VI.1249-55 (I) (*Comp.*, Supp.)
Bishop's Villa near Foligno: Old Bishop's Palace of Foligno; lateral façade of the Cathedral of Foligno.

VI.1987-96 (U) (*App.*)
Picture of Perseus and Andromeda: *Perseus and Andromeda*, the versions by Polidoro da Caravaggio and Volpato.

VII.186-92, 390-93 (I) (*Comp.*, Supp., *App.*)
Tapestry with mythological figures of Diana, Daphne, and Perseus: *Apollo and Daphne*, by Gerard Hoet; *Diana*, by Giambattista Tiepolo; *Perseus and Andromeda*, by Polidoro da Caravaggio, and the copy by Volpato.

IX.26-27, 120-30 (I) (Supp., *App.*)
Painting of the Holy Family slaughtered during the Flight into Egypt: *Holy Family with St. Anne*, *Slaughter of the Innocents*, by Mazzolino; *Flight into Egypt*, by Gaudenzio Ferrari.

IX.965-70 (U) (*Comp.*, *App.*)
Bas-relief of the legend of Hesione: *Perseus and Andromeda*, by both Polidoro da Caravaggio and Volpato; unspecified relief from antiquity representing Hesione chained to a rock.

Sor,   **I.567-83 (U)** (*Comp.*)
Sculpture representing Christ by Nicola Pisano: *Descent from the Cross*, a lunette on the façade of the Church of San Martino, Lucca; reliefs of the Crucifixion from the pulpits in the Baptistry of Pisa and the Duomo of Siena.

Up,   **26-30 (I)** (*Comp.*)
Fountain in Italy representing a nude woman and sea horses: *Fountain of Good Fortune*, Fano; *Birth of Venus*, by Botticelli; *Fountain of Neptune*, Trent, by Giongo; *Fountain of Neptune*, Florence, by Ammannati; *Fountain of Trevi*, Rome.

56-57 (U) (Supp.)
Villa representing the title of the poem: Villa Brichieri-Colombo, Florence; Villa Poggio al Vento, Marciano (environs of Siena); Casa Tolomei, Bagni di Lucca.

CORRECTIONS AND REVISIONS

The effect of the Doctrine of the Imperfect, as foreseen in the Notice to the *Compendium*, came to pass when the *Compendium* was published in 1991. Owing to the accretion of new findings, the desire to protect the findings by putting them in print as soon as possible, the pressure of a long-delayed publishing schedule, and my own inexperience under these conditions, I omitted circulating the manuscript among my readers for a second time after a hiatus of about two years following the first collective reading. The result was a product that reached my standard for originality and comprehensiveness of content but fell short of my expectation for correctness and consistency of form.

The following list represents the second collective effort of my readers and myself after closely examining the *Compendium* in its published form. It addresses the problems of correctness and consistency in the *Compendium*, though some changes are also included among the Citations and Notes of this appendix.

This section makes the *Compendium* more accurate and useful. Its inclusion explains why the *Compendium* has been withheld from review since 1991 and is now being released to reviewers only in tandem with this appendix.

At the beginning of this list, the words "Correction" and "Revision," as headings, should be distinguished from each other: corrections replace errors; revisions are improvements, not corrections for errors.

The reader will note that because of the recurrence of "fleur-de-lis" and "Grand Duke Ferdinand I" as corrections they are listed in their erroneous and corrected form only when they initially occur.

Page	Line(s)	Error or Revision Needed	Correction or Revision
x	17	Ormand	Ormond
	37	photographers Mr.	photographers, Mr.

xi	10	Fig.	Figs.
xii	23	,Joseph M.	,Mr. and Mrs. Joseph M.
1	3	greatest	largest
2	23	by Porter and Clarke	[omit]
	36	*fleur-de-lis*	fleur-de-lis
3	5	*a*	*A*
	16	*Universelle*	*universelle*
5	6	*Duke Ferdinand I*	*Grand Duke Ferdinand I*
6	19	signs	sign
9	2	*A Child*	*Child*
11	1	*Racers' Frieze*	*Procession of Horsemen*
12	12,13	Villa	Castle
14	1	a fresco by Gozzoli	detail of a fresco by Gozzoli
	2	Gelderin	Gelder
	13	Nuove	Nuovi
15	7	Raffaelle	Raffaello
18	13	Residence	Residenz
	15,20	Tiepolo	Giambattista Tiepolo
19	8	*Portrait*	*Sketch*
21	36	left arm	right arm
23	32-33	left hand	left-hand
26	17	(DEL,383;RIO,217)	(DEL,383;RIO,216-17)
	22	when	whom
	41	close	[omit]
30	12	new	New

32	24	painting	painter
34	2	the	[omit]
44	37	identify the "lump. . ."	identify the model for the "lump. . ."
55	11,16	Rifubbri	Refubbri
65	27	[see Cle, 174-80, above under Citations and Notes]	
73	40	Holy-water	holy-water
79	1	**AN**	**THE**
	38	west	southwest
81	10	An	The
95	5,9	Church	Monastery
	6	church	monastery
102	6	*among*	*between*
	14	*Among*	*between*
111	19	Walter	Waltraub
119	3	*The Temptation*	*The Temptation* (before restoration)
121	30	*Abate*	*Abbot*
123	43	line 346	line 377
124	10	Charmichael	Carmichael
134	11	La Banclocque	La Bancloche
143	16	Falconiere	Falconieri
	21	*Universelle*	*universelle*
146	14	Fig. 73	[omit from line 14 and put in line 18 before Map F:9G]
	24	spring	sprig
	34	T. Agnew and Sons	Thos. Agnew & Sons

150	4	T. Agnew and Sons	Thos. Agnew & Sons
161	3	by Rev. John	by the Rev. John
169		[see "The 'Moses' of Michael Angelo" above under Citations and Notes]	
171	27	*Universelle*	*universelle*
173	23,35	emmisary	emissary
	34	to officially receive	to receive officially
177	42	If the statuette was	[omit these words]
179	1-5	[poor logic]	[omit all five lines]
	23	pertinant	pertinent
181	20	highly probable	possible
	35	Tiepolo's	Giambattista Tiepolo's
182	2-3	identified with	associated with
	6	vividly fix	fix vividly
	25	1667	1672
185	38	Apollyan	Apollyon
193	7	agis	aegis
191	2	*Racers' Frieze*	*Procession of Horsemen*
195	24	Fréres	Frères
199	4	Gemäldagalerie	Gemäldegalerie
	6	Collections	Collection
	7	Kaiser Friedrich	Kaiser-Friedrich
212	38-39	Villa Torre al Gallo	Torre del Gallo
217	23	PARLEYINGS	PARLEYING
	33	in Mugello	in the Mugello
224	8	heaven / Resting	heaven, / Resting

	39	not little insight	no little insight
227	10	Hazlett	Hazlitt
229	9	research in the last century	more recent research
	20	Nostra	Mostra
	23	(STU, 23)	(STU, 23; EISE)
234	9	Villa	Castle
235	14	Villa	Castle
241	30	palace	castle
	33	Villa	Castle
245	28	his trips	his early trips
249	2	Balduchin	Baldachin
253	2	Cà	Ca'
257	2,9,11	book	novel
	6	looked up and saw a simple Etruscan ring, with	[delete "up" and comma]
262	11	Piazza di Santa Trinita	Piazza Santa Trinita
264	8	Piazza di Santa Trinita	Piazza Santa Trinita
274	8	and VII.394-96	[omit these words]
	32	(Map R:7I)	(Map R:7I; Figs. 154, 155)
277	24	*Honenstiel-Schwangau*	*Hohenstiel-Schwangau*
280	3	*Procession of the Kings*	*Procession of the Kings* (detail)
281	8	Gelderin	Gelder
282	2	Gelderin	Gelder
287	31	Wheron	Whereon

292	28	Arrezo	Arezzo
295	13	Also see under VII.394-96.	Also see above under I.780-84
298	3	theatre	theater
300	2	Nuove	Nuovi
306	7	Browning	Browning's
	21	, and 228	[omit]
	29,30	VI.668-73	VI.667-73
	40	imaginery	imaginary
308	18	scorpian	scorpion
311	25	misfortunately	[omit]
318	12,19	Santa Flora and Lucina	Sante Flora and Lucilla
321	23,25	Raffaelle	Raffaello
322	2	Raffaelle	Raffaello
330	12	portentious	portentous
335	11	Via "Corso"	Via del "Corso"
343	13	Parleyings	Parleying
360	37	"Camera"	*"Camera"*
	42,43	*Descrizione . . .Raefaello*	*Descrizzione* [sic] *. . .Rafaelle* [sic]
377	19	168	169
380	3	*The Expulsion*	*The Expulsion* (before restoration)
390	3	Prassade	Prassede
398	2	Tiepolo	Giambattista Tiepolo
402	2	Tiepolo	Giambattista Tiepolo
408	2	Fountain of Trevi	*Fountain of Trevi*
416	2	Ceiling of the Master Bedroom	Ceiling of the Master Bedroom (detail)

418	30	*Citta'*	*Città*
420	2	Heaven	heaven
	3	new	New
	30	to each paint	each to paint
421	3	winks	winks. . . .
	8	presumably flew	according to legend angels flew
	8	Narareth	Nazareth
	14	*Lavangro*	*Lavengro*
	14,25,27	Barrow	Borrow
	25	Barrow's	Borrow's
422	30	solidify	liquefy
423	17	feet	foot
	18	in the	to a
424	33	[see Cle, 174-80, above under Citations and Notes]	
425	1,12	King Cleon	King Protus
	19	consistant	consistent
	20	riprisals	reprisals
426	18	Domenicans	Dominicans
429	28	Lippi	Lippi's
430	27	nearby	near
431	22	Devane	DeVane
	26	Heaven	heaven
	29	Harriot	Harriet
432	6,8,15,16	Villa Brichieri	Villa Brichieri-Colombo
	21	Up at the Villa	Up at a Villa

	41	succeeds / to	succeeds to
434	5-7	[see Old, 26:201-02, above under Citations and Notes]	
435	1	Frà	Fra
438	7	Museum	Musée
	16	than	from
439	8	Harriot	Harriet
	14	1861	1864
	15	eight	eleven
441	8	, ay,	,--ay,
	11	,Riccardi,	,--Riccardi,
	40	frescoe	fresco
	41	stewart	steward
443	3,9	wedgewood	wedgwood
	5	half angel, half bird	half angel and half bird
	14	. . . one child	. . . one child,
444	32	fringe	frieze
445	16	Tiepolo's	Giambattista Tiepolo's
446	26-27	[add commas after "Guido," " Samson," and "Pompilia"]	
447	5	Bottinus's	Bottinius's
	21-22	Church of the Minorites	Church of Santa Maria delle Grazie
448	12	influenced	attracted
	21,26	Bottinus	Bottinius
451-57		[see Summary of Composite Sources above]	
458-64		[see Index of Artists below]	
465-96		[see Index of Sources with Locations below]	

497-502   [see Index of Miscellaneous Sources below]

503-521   [see Key to Bibliography below]

INDEX OF ARTISTS

This index supplements, revises, and corrects the Index of Artists given in the *Compendium*, pages 458-464. Only names of painters, sculptors, and architects that are specifically mentioned or obviously implied in Browning's poems are listed in this index. These names follow the form given in the Thieme-Becker *Lexikon* and/or the Bénézit *Dictionnaire*. The poems and line numbers in which the names are mentioned are listed under each of the names. The line numbers are taken from *A Concordance to the Poems of Robert Browning*, by Leslie N. Broughton and Benjamin F. Stelter (New York: Stechert, 1924-25). For the other systems of line numbering used in this study, see the *Compendium*, page 2. Not all the entries, it will be noted, are mentioned or discussed in either the *Compendium* or this appendix.

CLASSICAL (6th and 5th centuries B.C.)
    Greek
        Phidias
            "Cleon," 141

MEDIEVAL (13th and 14th centuries)
    Italian
        Cimabue, Giovanni Gualtieri
            "Old Pictures in Florence," 180
        Dello Delli, or Dello di Niccolò Delli ("Dellos")
            "Old Pictures in Florence," 64
        Fra Angelico, or Fra Giovanni da Fiesole
            "Fra Lippo Lippi," 235
            "Old Pictures in Florence," 204
            The Ring and the Book, XI.2114
        Gaddi, Taddeo
            "Old Pictures in Florence," 205

RENAISSANCE (15th and 16th centuries)
    Italian (cont.)
        Titian, or Tiziano Vecelli ("Tizian") (cont.)
           "Cenciaja," 22
           "Filippo Baldinucci on the Privilege of Burial," 402, 419,
               439
           "Founder of the Feast," 3
           "How It Strikes a Contemporary," 76
           "In a Gondola," 193
           Pippa Passes, III.163
           The Ring and the Book, XI.2114
        Vasari, Giorgio
           "Andrea del Sarto," 106
           "Old Pictures in Florence," 72

BAROQUE (17th century)
    Flemish
        Rubens, Peter Paul
           In a Balcony, 130, 677
    French
        Du Pré, Abraham
           The Two Poets of Croisic, 377
        Daret, Pierre
           The Two Poets of Croisic, 378
    Italian
        Albano, Francesco
           The Ring and the Book, XI.270
        Bernini, Gian Lorenzo
           The Ring and the Book, I.891
        Buti, Lodovico
           "Filippo Baldinucci on the Privilege of Burial," 53ff
        Carracci, Annibale
           Pippa Passes (Porter and Clarke, I, 320, identify the
              reference in Act I, line 412, to "Hannibal Scratchy" as
              a play on Carracci's name)
        Dolci, Carlo ("Carlino")
           "Old Pictures in Florence," 232
           The Ring and the Book, III.58, IX.34
        Ferri, Ciro
           The Ring and the Book, V.487, IX.117
        Furini, Francesco
           "Parleying with Francis Furini," 1ff

ROMANTIC (19th century)
  French
    Corot, Jean-Baptiste Camille
      The Inn Album, I.77
    Doré, Gustave
      Fifine at the Fair, 551, 571
    Gérôme, Jean-Léon
      Fifine at the Fair, 709
    Meissonier, Jean-Louis-Ernest
      Red Cotton Night-Cap Country, IV.772
    Pradier, Jean Jacques, called James
      Prince Hohenstiel-Schwangau, 186
  Italian
    Ademollo, Luigi
      The Ring and the Book, I.364

VICTORIAN (19th century)
  English
    Barry, Sir Charles
      The Inn Album, III.7
    Gibson, John
      "Youth and Art," 8, 55
    Hunt, William Holman (his painting, "Light o' the World")
      The Inn Album, I.37
    Landseer, Sir Edwin Henry
      The Inn Album, I.35
    Leighton, Frederic (Lord) ("Kaunian Painter")
      Balaustion's Adventure, 2672
      "Eurydice to Orpheus," 1-8
      "Parleying with Christopher Smart," 90
      "Yellow and pale as ripened corn," 1-4
    Millais, Sir John Everett (his painting, "Huguenot")
      The Inn Album, I.37
    Pugin, Augustus Welby
      "Bishop Blougram's Apology," 6
    Watts, George Frederick
      "Parleying with Christopher Smart," 91 (name identi-
        fied by PET, II, 1108n)
    Woolner, Thomas
      "Deaf and Dumb," 1-8

INDEX OF SOURCES WITH LOCATIONS

This index supplements, updates, and corrects the Index of Sources with Locations in the *Compendium*, pages 465-96. Unless *Appendix A* is indicated, all references below are to poems and line numbers in the *Compendium*. An asterisk after an entry indicates an original source nominated by the author. Abbreviations used in this index are the head letters indicating the titles of the poems covered in this study and the numbers indicating the line numbers of the citations from the poems (*e.g.*, And, 1-3, means "Andrea del Sarto," lines 1-3).

AUSTRIA
    Innsbruck
        Court Church
            Bronze statues of König Albrecht I (Fig. 292) and Kaiser Friedrich III (Fig. 293)
                My, 54-56; *App. A*, My, 48-56 (*)
                Pip, II.49-55; *App. A*, Pip, II.49-51 (*)
    Vienna
        Albertina Museum
            Sketch for the *Disputa* with a sonnet, by Raphael
                One, 2:5-17

BELGIUM
    Mechelen
        Cathedral of St. Rombold (Fig. 66)
            How, 17

CANADA
    Toronto
        Mr. and Mrs. Joseph Tanenbaum
            Hercules Wrestling with Death for the Body of Alcestis, a painting by Leighton (Fig. 7)
            Bal, 2672-97

ENGLAND (cont.)
  London (cont.)
    Leighton House
      Orpheus and Eurydice, a painting by Lord Leighton
      (Fig. 36)
        Eur, 1-8; *App. A*, same citation
    National Gallery
      Adoring Saints, from the *San Benedetto Altarpiece*, by
      Lorenzo Monaco (Fig. 283)
        Old, *App. A*, 26:205-08
      Pan Pursuing Syrinx, a painting by Hendrick van Balen
      Bis, 56-61 (*)
      Seven Saints, Sacred Conversation, a painting by Filip-
      po Lippi (Fig. 45)
        Fra, 47-49, 245-46
      Trinity and Saints, a painting by Filippo Lippi
        Fra, 70-75 (*)
      Trinity and Saints, a painting by Filippo Lippi and
      Pesellino
        Fra, 145-63 (*)
    National Portrait Gallery
      Bronze cast of the clasped hands of the Brownings, by
      Harriet Hosmer
        Jam, VIII.27-32 (*), IX.18-20 (see Pro, 27-28)
        Lik, 49-50
        Pro, 27-28 (*)
    St. George's Cathedral, Southwark (Fig. 11)
        Bi, 3-9 (*)
    St. Margaret's Church
        Jub, 1-4
    St. Paul's Cathedral
      Bell-tower
        Tim, 22
      The Light of the World, a painting by William Hol-
      man Hunt (Fig. 77)
        Inn, I.34-37
    Henry Sotheran & Co., book dealers
      Giorgio Vasari's *Lives*, 1846-57 Italian edition, copy
      owned by Browning, *Portrait of Margheritone*, by
      Spinello Aretino (Fig. 254)
        Old, 28:217-21

ENGLAND (cont.)
  Windsor
    Windsor Castle, Royal Library
      Two Hands, a sketch by Leonardo da Vinci (Fig. 82)
        Jam, VIII.71-76 (*)
  Yorkshire
    Harewood House
      Christ at the Column, a painting attributed to the school of Antonio Pollaiuolo (Fig. 101)
        Old, 27:209-16

FRANCE
  Avon
    Parish Church (Fig. 29)
      Tomb of the Marquis Monaldeschi (Fig. 30)
        Cri, 121-28
  Fontainebleau
    Fontainebleau Palace (Fig. 24)
      Diane de Poitier Asks Grace from Francis I for Her Father, a painting by Madame Haudebourg-Lescot (Fig. 27)
        Cri, 81-88 (*)
      Crescent and salamander decor (Figs. 25 and 26)
        Cri, 5-14ff (*)
      Gallery of the Deer (Fig. 28)
        Cri, 105-12
  La Délivrande
    Basilica (Fig. 139)
      Red
  Montpellier
    Musée Fabre
      Sketch for the *Disputa* with a sonnet, by Raphael
        One, 2:5-17
  Paris
    Bibliothèque Nationale
      The Morgue, a drawing by Meryon (Fig. 6)
        App, 1-3, 10-11
    Church of the Madeleine
      Marriage of the Virgin, a statue by James Pradier
        Pri, 194-96 (*)
    Garde-Meuble
      Life of Christ, copies of tapestries by Raphael
        Pri, 850-55

GERMANY (cont.)
Berlin (cont.)
  Staatliche Museen, Gemäldegalerie (cont.)
    Leda and the Swan, a painting by Correggio (Fig. 78)
      Inn, I.392-93
      Rin, IV.888-89
    Venus with the Organ-Player, a painting by Titian
      Any, 77-78 (*)
Bremen
  Kunsthalle
    Psiche-Fanciulla, a statue by Canova (Fig. 129)
      Pip, I.375-94
Dresden
  Staatliche Kunstsammlungen
    Sistine Madonna, a painting by Raphael (Fig. 109)
      One, 3:18-25
Füssen
  Hohen-Schwangau Castle (Fig. 294)
    Pri, title, *App. A*
Hamelin
  Bungelosestrasse
    Pie, 277-88 (*)
  New Market Place
    Pie, 216-17 (*)
Munich
  Alte Pinakothek
    Madonna of the Palazzo Tempi, a painting by Raphael
    (Fig. 4)
      And, 103-12
    St. Michael, a painting by Mabuse (Berneart van Orley)
      Bi, 666-68 (*)
  Glyptothek
    Paris, a statue from the Aeginetan Sculptures (Fig. 96)
      Old, 13:97-104
  Residenz
    Treasury Room
    Neptune, a 16th-century chalice (Fig. 240)
      My, 54-56 (*); *App. A*, My, 48-56
    Neptune Vase (cat. no. 328, Neptune surmounting an
    ornate vase and holding a trident); not discussed in
    Comp. or *App. A*
      My, 54-56 (*)

GREECE
   Athens
      Stoa Poecile ("Poikilé")
         Bal, 2672-97
         Cle, 51-54

HUNGARY
   Budapest
      Academy of Fine Arts
         Venus Mourning the Death of Adonis, a painting by
         Francesco Furini (Fig. 284)
            Par, *App. A*, 2:76-96 (*)

IRELAND
   Clandeboye
      Tower of Lady Helen Dufferin (Fig. 64)
         Hel, 12-13

ITALY
   Abano
      Archeological Zone
         Fountain of Tiberius (ruins)
            Piet, *App.A*, 55:436-38
   Arezzo
      Bishop's Palace (Fig. 172)
         Rin, VII.757
      Cathedral
         Grand Duke Ferdinand I, a statue by Giovanni da
         Bologna (Fig. 172)
            Cle, 174-80 (*); *App. A*, Cle, 174-76
            Rin, VI.249-56
         Life of Christ, stained-glass windows by Guillaume de
         Marcillat
            Rin, VI.460-62
         Madonna and Child, a relief on the monument for St.
         Donatus, by Betto di Francesco and Giovanni di
         Francesco (Fig. 224)
            Rin, VI.400-406, 667-73 (*); *App. A*, Rin, VI.400-06,
            667-73, 913-14
      Chimera of Arezzo (two bronze copies in the park in front
      of the railroad station)
         Rin, XI.1115-26; *App. A*, Rin, XI.184-88

ITALY (cont.)
  Arezzo (cont.)
    Church of the Abbey of Sante Flora and Lucilla
      St. George and the Dragon, a painting by Vasari
      (Fig. 180)
        Rin, VII.1323-28
    Church of the Pieve
      Crypt, *Virgin of Sorrows*, a statue by Raynaldo Barto-
      lini (Fig. 227)
        Rin, VI.702-07
      Façade (Fig. 173)
        Rin, VI.345-48, 974-76
    Church of San Francesco
      Triumph of St. Michael, a fresco by Spinello Aretino
      (Fig. 179)
        Rin, VII.1215-19
    Governor's Palace
        Rin, VII.1255-56
    Logge Vasari (Salone delle Commedie, a former theater;
    not discussed)
        Rin, II.801, IV.944, VI.395, VII.958
    Porta San Clemente
        Rin, V.1022-29, VI.1080-83
    Porta Santo Spirito (Fig. 171)
        Rin, V.1022-29
    Torrione (Fig. 170)
        Rin, V.1022-29, VI.1080-83
    Via de'Cenci
        Rin, II.471-72
  Asolo
    Castle of Catherine Cornaro (Figs. 126, 127)
        Inap, *App. A*, 3-4, 12-13
        Pip, II.271-74
    Cathedral (Fig. 128)
        Pip, Intro., 180-82, I.58-61
    La Rocca (Castle of Asolo) (Fig. 126)
        Inap, *App. A*, 3-4, 12-13
        Pip, Intro., 171-73
    Palazzo Governo (Fig. 127)
        Pip, Intro., 180-82

ITALY (cont.)
  Fano
    Civic Museum
      The Guardian Angel, a painting by Guercino (Fig. 62)
        Gua, 36-37
    Piazza 20 Settembre
      Fountain of Good Fortune (Fig. 218)
        Up, 26-30 (*)
  Ferrara
    Bastione di S. Tommaso
      Sor, IV.533-35, V.282-85
    Church of San Pietro, formerly (Fig. 205)
      Sor, IV.157-71
    Este Castle (Fig. 90)
      My, 47-48
    Palace of San Pietro (former site)
      Sor, IV.157-71
  Florence
    Baptistery (Map F:7H), *Creation of Eve,* a bronze door
    panel by Ghiberti (Fig. 56)
      Fra, 265-69 (*)
    Bell-tower (Map F:7H; Fig. 106)
      Old, 35:278-89, 36:281-88
   Bridges
    Ponte alla Carraia (Map F:8G)
      Fra, 90-91
    Ponte Santa Trinita (Map F:8G; Fig. 145)
      Rin, I.110-16
   Cemeteries
    Jewish, 16 Viale L. Ariosto (Map F:8F; Fig. 230)
      Fil, 31:241-44ff
    Protestant, Piazza Donatello, tomb of Elizabeth Barrett
    Browning (Fig. 37)
      Eur, 1-8 (*); *App. A,* same citation
      Flu, *App. A,* 46-48 (*)
      Parl, *App. A,* 16:426-34
      Rin, *App. A,* I.1-4, 15-17 (*)
   Churches, Convents, and Monasteries
    Certosa (Fig. 183)
      Rin, XI.3-14
    Ognissanti (Map F:7G; Fig. 103)
      Old, 31:241-43

ITALY (cont.)
  Florence (cont.)
    Museums (cont.)
      Archeological Museum (Map F:6I)
        Chimera of Arezzo, a bronze sculpture (Fig. 188)
            Rin, XI.1115-25; *App. A*, Rin, XI.184-88
      Bargello (National Museum) (Map F:8H,8I; Fig. 86, middle
      tower)
            Lur, I.297-300
        Portrait of Dante, a detail of a fresco attributed to
        Giotto; sketch of the same by Seymour Kirkup (Figs.
        209, 210)
            Old, 24:185-92
            Sou, verso of title page (*)
      Museo dell'Opera del Duomo (Map F:7I)
        A design of the Bell-tower of Florence, attributed to
        Giotto (Fig. 106)
            Old, 35:278-80, 36:281-88
      Palazzo Pitti (Map F:9G)
        Adam and Eve in Earthly Paradise, a painting by Fran-
        cesco Furini (Fig. 285); paintings about Lorenzo the
        Magnificent by Furini
            Par, *App. A*, 2:76-96, 3:152-60
            Rin, *App. A*, I.38, 45-49 (*)
        La Velata, a painting by Raphael (Fig. 108)
            One, 2:5-17
        Lucrezia de'Medici, a painting by Bronzino (Fig. 222)
            My, 1-4
        Madonna and Child and the Life of St. Anne, a paint-
        ing by Filippo Lippi (Fig. 51)
            Fra, 145-63
        Madonna del Granduca, a painting by Raphael (Fig.
        111)
            One, 3:18-25
            Pa, *App. A*, 3:40-44 (*)
            Rin, VI.400-06, 667-73 (*); *App. A*, Rin, VI.400-06,
            667-73, 913-14
        Portrait of a Man and a Woman, a painting once
        attributed o Andrea del Sarto (Fig. 1)
            And, 1-3

ITALY (cont.)
  Florence (cont.)
    Squares (cont.)
      Piazza della Signoria (Map F:8H; Fig. 86)
          Lur, I.67-73 (Palazzo Vecchio)
          Old, 33:260-63 (Loggia, by Orcagna)
          Up, 26-30 (*Neptune Fountain*, by Ammannati) (*)
      Piazza San Lorenzo (Map F:7H)
          John of the Black Bands, a statue on a pedestal by
          Baccio Bandinelli (Figs. 140, 141, 257)
          Rin, 38-52 (*), 91-95; *App. A*, Rin, I.38, 45-49 (*)
      Piazza Santissima Annunziata (Map F:7I)
          Grand Duke Ferdinand I, an equestrian statue by Gio-
          vanni da Bologna (Figs. 2, 213, 214)
              Sta, 199-202
    Street
      Borgo Allegri (Map F:8I)
              Pic, 25-26, 31-38
    Tower
      Torre del Gallo
              One, 16:164 (*)
  Foligno
    Duomo
      Romanesque portal with eagles and serpentine figures,
      on the lateral façade (Figs. 242 and 243)
              Rin, VI.1249-55 (*)
      Old Bishop's Palace (Fig. 242)
              Rin, VI.1249-55 (*)
  Galli Islands, Amalfian Coast
    Tower of Robert of Naples (Fig. 32)
              Eng, 207-38; *App. A*, Eng, 207-18
  Goito
    Castle (ruins)
              Sor, I.381-82
  Loreto
    Santuario della Santa Casa
      Life of the Virgin, marble panels by Andrea Sansovino
              Bi, 377 (*)
    Museo della Santa Casa
      Life of Christ, copies of the tapestries by Raphael
              Pri, 850-55 (*)

ITALY (cont.)
Nemi
Temple of Diana (ruins); model of the temple in the
Museo delle Navi Romane
Pri, *App. A*, 1986-97
Padua
Duomo (Fig. 79)
Ita, 73-75
Governor's Palace ("Podestà")
Sor, I.150
Palermo
Palazzina Cinese (Fig. 202)
Sor, III.119-21
Palazzo della Zisa
Sor, III.119-21 (*)
Parma
National Art Gallery
Virgin with St. Jerome and Mary Magdalen, a painting
by Correggio (Fig. 12)
Bi, 113-17, 704-07 (*)
Piano di Sorrento
Church of the Santissima Trinità (Fig. 34) (*); Mount
Vicoalvano (Fig. 35)
Madonna of the Rosary, an effigy (Fig. 33)
Eng, 260-91 (*)
Pisa
Baptistery
Crucifixion, a relief on the pulpit, by Nicola Pisano
Sor, I.567-83
Bell-tower (Leaning Tower)
One, 16:164
Camposanto
Triumph of Death, a fresco by the Master of the Tri-
umph of Death (Fig. 244)
Fra, 183-93
Poggio a Caiano
Villa Medicea (Fig. 268)
Caesar Presented with Tribute, a painting in the Sala
Grande, by Andrea del Sarto (Fig. 269)
And, 259-63 (*); *App. A*, same citation

ITALY (cont.)
  Rome (cont.)
    Castel Sant'Angelo (cont.)
        Cen, 228-30
        Rin, I.350-60, 1284-85, X.1010-12, 2106-11, XII.159-65;
            App. A, X.1010-12
        Sor, IV.1014-22
    Churches
    Capuchins (Map R:6I; Fig. 153)
        Rin, I.896-903; *App. A*, Rin, XI.184-88
    Gesù (Map R:8H; Fig. 160); Chapel of St. Ignatius Loyola
    (Figs. 272, 273)
        Bis, 42-49; *App. A*, Bis, 42, 47-49
        Rin, III.103-04
    Gesù e Maria (Map R:6H)
        Rin, III.35-37
    San Giovanni in Laterano (Fig. 178)
        Rin, VII.262-63
    San Lorenzo in Lucina (Map R:6H; Fig. 152)
      Crucifixion, a painting by Guido Reni (Fig. 158);
      LionStatues (Figs. 176, 177)
        Rin, I.874-76, II.83-96, VII.21-27, 425-30; *App. A*, Rin,
            XI.184-88
    San Pietro in Vincoli; *Moses*, a statue by Michelangelo
    (Fig. 88)
        Bi, 425 ("Peter's Chains")
        Mos, 1-14; *App. A*, same citation
    Sant'Agnese in Agone (Map R:7G; Figs. 194, 195)
        Rin, XII.159-65
    Sant'Angelo in Pescheria (Map R:8H; Fig. 65)
        Hol, 2:12
    Sant'Anna
        Rin, III.35-37
    Santa Maria del Popolo (Figs. 147, 148)
        Rin, I.350-60
    Santa Maria d'Aracoeli (Map R:8I; Fig. 69)
      Altar to Augustus (Fig. 70)
        Imp, 139-42, 157-60
    Santa Maria della Rotonda ("Pantheon"; Map R:7H; Fig.
    169)
        Rin, V.703-05, XII.138-46

ITALY (cont.)
  Rome (cont.)
    Conservatori Museum (cont.)
      Chr, *App. A*, Pt. I, 12:749-52, 764-68 (*)
      Prot, 55-57 (*); *App. A*, Prot, 52-57
     Temple of Jupiter ("Thundering Jupiter") (ruins)
      Imp, 31-40, 92-94, 100-01
    Roma (Map R:8G)
     Perseus and Andromeda, a fresco by Polidoro da Cara-
     vaggio (Fig. 121)
      Fif, *App. A*, sections 47 (*) and 49 (*)
      Pau, 656-67; *App. A*, same citation
      Rin, VII.390-93, IX.965-70; *App. A*, Rin, VI.1987-96
        (*), VII.390-93, IX.965-70
    Villa Giulia
     13th-century fleur-de-lis ring in collection of Castellani
     jewelry (Fig. 258, dust-cover, and half-title page; *App.*
     A, dust-cover and half-title page)
      Rin, I.1-4, 15-17 (*); *App. A*, same citation
  Palaces
    Barberini (Map R:7H)
     La Fornarina, a painting by Raphael (Fig. 231)
      One, 2:5-17
    Bufalo (Map R:7H; Fig. 123)
      Pau, 656-67
    Castellani (Map. R:7I; Fig. 251)
      Rin, 1-4, 15-17; *App. A*, same citation
    Cenci (Map R:8H; Fig. 21)
      Cen, 266-69
    Corsini (Map R:8F)
     Beatrice Cenci, a painting attributed to Guido Reni (Fig.
     19)
      Cen, 15-29 (*); *App. A*, same citation
    Farnese (Map R:8G; Fig. 191)
      Rin, XII.110-11
    Fiano (Map R:6H)
      Rin, I.874-76
    Orsini (Map R:8H; Fig. 20)
      Cen, 266-69
    Ruspoli (Map R:6H)
      Rin, I.874-76

ITALY (cont.)
  Rome (cont.)
   Streets
    Babuino (Map R:6H)
     Rin, II.200-07, III.388-93
    Bocca di Leone, Browning's residence (Map R:6H)
     Rin, VII.425-30
    Corso (Map R:6H,7H,8H; Fig. 196)
     Hol, 9:52
     Rin, VII.425-30, XII.138-46
    Convertite (Map R:7H)
     Rin, II.1229-31, VIII.1064
    Giulia (Map R:7F,8F)
     Rin, XII.138-46
    Governo (Map R:7G)
     Rin, XII.138-46
    Lungara (Map R:8F)
     Rin, II.1229-31
    Pellegrino ("Pilgrim"; Map R:8F,8G)
     Rin, XII.138-46
    Tor di Nona (Map R:7F,7G)
     Cen, 175-77
     Rin, I.1284-85, V.324-25, XII.138-48, 159-65
    Vittoria (Map R:6H)
     Rin, II.200-07, XII.138-46
   Theater
    Theater of Marcellus (Map R:8H,9H; Fig. 20)
     Cen, 266-69
     Imp, 31-40
  San Marino
   Rocca Guàita (Fig. 234)
    Gra, 13-20 (*); *App A, Gra,* 13-16
  Siena
   Church of St. John's Observance (Fig. 116)
    Pac, 17:307-09
   Church of the Servites
    Lady of Sorrows, an effigy (Fig. 220)
     Up, 51-52 (*)
   Duomo and Square of the Duomo (Fig. 22)
    Pac, 14:233-37
    Crucifixion, a relief on the pulpit in the Duomo, by
    Nicola Pisano (Fig. 199)
     Sor, 567-84 (*)

ITALY (cont.)
  Treviso (cont.)
    Duomo
      Annunciation, a painting by Titian (Fig. 131)
        Pip, III.162-63
  Trieste
    Piazza della Borsa
      Neptune, a statue by Mazzolan da Bergamo (Fig. 221)
        My, 54-56 (*); *App. A*, My, 48-56
  Turin
    Accademia Albertini
      Four Fathers of the Church, a painting by Filippo Lippi
        Fra, 70-75 (*)
    Palazzo Rivoli (environs; Fig. 83)
        Kin, stage directions
    Piazza Carlina (Carlo Emanuele II)
        Kin, II.77-79
  Urbino
    Palazzo Ducale
      Life of Christ, copies of tapestries by Raphael
        Pri, 850-55 (*)
  Vallombrosa
    Monastery of Vallombrosa
        Rin, XI.902-09
  Varallo
    Church of Santa Maria delle Grazie (correction of Mrs.
    Jameson by Professor Eisenberg)
      Flight into Egypt, a fresco by Gaudenzio Ferrari (Fig.
      298)
        Rin, IV.420-25 (*), IX.26-27, 120-30 (*); *App. A*, Rin,
          I.1-4, 15-17
  Vatican
    Basilica of St. Peter
      Baldachin (Fig. 134)
        Chr, 10:526-76
      Colonnade (Fig. 133)
        Boy, 47-52
        Chr, 10:526-76
        Pri, 861-65
      Dome (Fig. 133)
        Abt, 13-24
        Chr, 10:526-76
        Eas, 26:798-802
        Pri, 861-65

ITALY (cont.)
   Venice (cont.)
      Ducal Palace (Figs. 201, 204, 216) (*)
         Neptune, a statue by Jacopo Sansovino (Fig. 201) (*);
         Venice Receives the Homage of Neptune, a painting by
         Giambattista Tiepolo (Fig. 241) (*)
            My, 54-56; *App. A*, My, 48-56
      Naval Museum
         Small model of *Bucentaur* (Fig. 299)
            Toc, 5-8 (*); *App. A*, same citation
      Piazza San Bartolommeo
         Statue of Goldoni (Fig. 61)
            Gold, 1-2
      Piombi (prisons) (Fig. 204)
         Sor, III.876-77; *App. A*, Toc, 5-8
      Ponte dell'Angelo, Palazzo Soranzo, marble relief on
      façade (Fig. 132)
         Pon, 7-12
      Rialto Bridge (Fig. 217)
         Toc, 5-8
      Teatro la Fenice
         Pip, I.417
   Verona
      Church of Sant'Eufemia, sacristy
         Sor, I.567-83
      Piazza delle Erbe
         Madonna of Verona, a fountain statue (Fig. 203)
            Sor, III.586-87
   Vicenza
      Governor's Palace ("Podestà")
         Sor, I.535
   Viterbo
      Romanelli House (Fig. 9)
         Bea, 306-15 (*)

RUSSIA
   Moscow
      The Kremlin
         Kolokol Bell (Fig. 80)
            Iva, 414-18, 421-25

UNITED STATES (cont.)
   Cambridge, Massachusetts (cont.)
      Radcliffe College
         Original plaster cast of the clasped hands of the Brownings, by Harriet Hosmer
            Jam, VIII.27-32 (*), IX.18-20 (see Pro, 27-28)
            Pro, 27-28 (*)
   Claremont, California
      Scripps College
         Plaster cast of the clasped hands of the Brownings, by Harriet Hosmer
            Jam, VIII.27-32 (*), IX.18-20 (see Pro, 27-28)
            Pro, 27-28 (*)
   Columbus, Ohio
      Ohio Historical Society
         The Modern Art of Taming Wild Horses, by J. S. Rarey, the copy owned by Browning
            Lik, 22-23
   Detroit, Michigan
      The Detroit Institute of Arts
         Neptune, a statuette by Jacopo Sansovino (Fig. 91)
            My, 54-56; *App. A*, My, 48-56
   Miami, Florida
      Vizcaya Museum
         Tapestry no. 1385 from the Browning collection (KEL, 524, item H667)
            Chi, 13:76-78
   New Haven, Connecticut
      Yale University Library
         The Art of Painting in All Its Branches, by Gerard de Lairesse, the copy owned by Robert Browning
            Bis, 68-69, 106-12, 116-17
            Chi
            Parl, *App. A*, 3:71-80 (Fig. 277) (*), 5:116-26 (Fig. 290) (*), 6:163-65 (Fig. 291) (*), 8:188-98 (Fig. 277) (*)
   New York, New York
      The Browning Institute (agent)
         Diamond Betrothal Ring of the Brownings (Fig. 252)
            Jam, VIII.43-48

UNITED STATES (cont.)
    Waco, Texas
        Armstrong Browning Library
            Bronze cast of the clasped hands of the Brownings, by
            Harriet Hosmer (Fig. 81)
                Jam, VIII.27-32 (*), IX.18-20 (see Pro, 27-28)
                Pro, 27-28 (*)
            The Delivery to the Secular Arm, a painting by Pen
            Browning (Fig. 197.5)
                Sc, 1-5
            Dryope, photographs of statues in plaster and bronze by
            Pen Browning (Fig. 286)
                Par, *App. A*, 3:152-60 (*)
                Parl, *App. A*, 5:116-26 (*)
            Eve after Temptation, a photograph of a plaster statue
            by Pen Browning (Fig. 289)
                Par, *App. A*, 3:152-60 (*)
                Parl, *App. A*, 5:116-26 (*)
            The Serenade, a painting by D. Maclise (Fig. 71)
                In, 1-7
            Wonders of the Little World, by Nathaniel Wanley,
            the copy owned by Browning
                My, 54-56
    Washington, District of Columbia
        National Gallery of Art
            Small Cowper Madonna, a painting by Raphael (Fig.
            228)
                Rin, VI.400-06, 667-73; *App. A*, Rin, VI.400-06, 667-
                73, 913-14
    Wellesley, Massachusetts
        Wellesley College, Clapp Library, Special Collections
            Bronze cast of the clasped hands of the Brownings, by
            Harriet Hosmer
                Jam, VIII.27-32 (*), IX.18-20 (see Pro, 27-28)
                Pro, 27-28 (*)
            Still Life of Fruits and Vegetables, a watercolor by Pen
            Browning (Fig. 288)
                Parl, *App. A*, 5:116-26 (*)

INDEX OF MISCELLANEOUS SOURCES

This index supplements, revises, and corrects the Index of Miscellaneous Sources in the *Compendium*, pages 497-502. Unless *Appendix A* is indicated, all references below are to poems and line numbers in the *Compendium*. An asterisk after an entry indicates an original source nominated by the author. Abbreviations used in this index are the head letters indicating the titles of the poems covered in this study and the numbers indicating the line numbers of the citations from the poems (*e.g.*, And, 1-3, means "Andrea del Sarto," lines 1-3).

Admollo, Luigi, unspecified prints, Rin, I.66-75, 369-72.

Andrea del Sarto, *Portrait of the Dauphin* (untraced), And, 148-51.

Aphrodite, unspecified statue of, Chr, Pt.I,11:678-82.

Arnold, Matthew, "Empedocles on Etna," *App. A*, Gra, 31-34 (*) (see below under Olympus).

Bacon, Roger, Brazen Head, Rin, VIII.985-87 (see below under Byron).

Baldinucci, Filippo, *Notizie*:
    Life of Andrea del Sarto, see DEVA, 245.
    Life of Artemisia Gentileschi, Bea, 17-24, 306-15.
    Life of Filippo Lippi, see DEVA, 217.
    Life of Francesco Furini, Par, 1:3-7.
    Life of Francesco Romanelli, Bea, 17-24, 306-15.
    Life of Lodovico Buti, Fil, 241-44ff.
    Life of Pacchiarotto, Pac, 5:64-75.

Bartoli, Daniel, *De'simboli transportati al morale*, Bis, 68-69.

Bellori, Giovanni Pietro, *Descrizzione* [sic] *delle imagini dipinte da Raffaelle* [sic] *d'Urbino nelle camere del Palazzo Apostolico Vaticano*, Sou.

Blagden, Isabella, *Agnes Tremorne*, Rin, I.1-4, 15-17.

Browning, Elizabeth Barrett, *Casa Guidi Windows*, Old, 33:257-58, 35:278-80, 36:281-88; Par, 3:176-81.

Browning, Robert, literary source for a picture of St. Jerome in "Fra Lippo Lippi," 70-75, see Bi, 704-07 (*).

Browning, Robert Wiedemann Barrett (Pen), private collections, *Dryope* (2) (**) and *Eve after Temptation* (*), *App. A*, Par, 3:152-60, Parl, 5:116-26 (Figs. 286 and 289). Also see the Index of Sources with Locations, under Armstrong Browning Library, Waco, Texas (Fig. 197.5); Wellesley College, Wellesley, Mass. (Fig. 288) (*); and Trask Family Estate, Saratoga Springs, New York (Fig. 287).

Brueghel, the Elder, *Pan Pursuing Syrinx* (untraced), Bis, 56-61 (see below under Rubens).

Buti, Lodovico, *Madonna* and *Crucifixion* (untraced), Fil, 31:241-44ff.

Byron, Lord, *Childe Harold's Pilgrimage*, IV, 1:1 and 8, 4:4-6, Sor, V.136-37, 876-77, Toc, 5-8, *App. A*, Toc, 5-8; *Don Juan*, I, stanza 217, Rin, VIII.985-87 (see above under Bacon). Particular appreciation for consultation and support is expressed to the Byron specialist Dr. Clement T. Goode, Professor of English at Baylor University.

Caponsacchi, Giuseppe, Florentine house of (general location), Rin, VI.231-34.

Comparini, Roman House of (destroyed), Rin, II.200-07, VII.77-81.

Diamond betrothal ring of the Brownings, private collection, Jam, VIII, 43-48, Rin, I.38, 45-49; *App. A*, Rin, I.38, 45-49 (*).

Kingsley, Charles, *Alton Locke, Yeast*, Fra, 286-90.

Lairesse, Gerard de, *The Art of Painting*, Bis, 68-69, 106-12, 116-17, Chi; *App. A*, Par, 3:152-6 (Fig. 29) (*), Parl, 3:71-80 (Fig. 277) (*), 5:116-26 (Fig. 290) (*), 6:163-65 (Fig. 291) (*), 8:188-98 (Fig. 277) (*).

Leicester Square, one imaginary and one destroyed statue in, Pri, 6-8, 194-96 (see above under George I).

Leighton, Lord, painting of Letty Dene (untraced), Yel, 1-4.

Lighthouse in Greece (unspecified), Cle, 51-54.

"Love Among the Ruins," general setting, Lov.

Lucrezia de'Medici, portrait paintings by Bronzino or Allori; portrait medals by Pastorino da Siena, Francesco Salviati, and Domenico Poggini, My, 54-56 (see *Comp.*, 171, for locations).

Margheritone d'Arezzo, *Crucifixion* (untraced), Old, 28:217-24.

Masaccio, Tommaso, *Consecration* (destroyed), Fra, 145-63.

Milton, John, *Paradise Lost*, Abt, 13-24 (*).

Moscheles, Felix, *The Isle's Enchantress* (untraced), Isl, 1-5.

Mote House, Bedford (destroyed), Ned, 278 (*).

Murray, John, ed., *Handbook for Travellers in Central Italy*, Bis, 56-61 (*); *Handbook for Travellers in Switzerland, and the Alps of Piedmont*, By, 14:66-68.

New Place, house of Shakespeare in Stratford-on-Avon (destroyed), Bi, 513-16.

Olympus, Mount, home of the Greek Gods, *App. A*, Gra, 31-34 (*) (see above under Arnold).

Pacchiarotto, Giacomo, house in Siena of (destroyed), Pac, 5: 64-75.

green-eyed monster imagery from *Othello* (literary source only), *App. A, For,* 271-77 (*).

Shelley, Mary, *Rambles in Germany and Italy in 1840, 1842, and 1843,* Old, 26:201-08.

Shelley, Percy B., *The Cenci,* Cen, 15-29; "Lines Written among the Euganean Hills," Ita, 73-75 (*); "Ode to the West Wind," *App. A,* Eur (*); "Ozymandias," *App. A,* Chr, Pt.I, 12:749-52, 764-68 (*).

Soccorso Gate, Turin (untraced), Kin, II.77-79.

Tapestries owned by the Brownings depicting Medici coats of arms (untraced), Rin, I.1-4, 15-17 (*).

Tomb of Elizabeth Barrett Browning, a photograph in a private collection, Parl, 16:6-14.

Tydeus, imaginary statue of, Pip, I.413-14.

Vasari, Giorgio, *Vite*:
  Life of Andrea del Castagno and Domenico Veneziano, Fra, 145-63 (*), 323-32.
  Life of Andrea del Sarto, And, 103-12.
  Life of Antonio Pollaiuolo, Old, 27:209-16.
  Life of Baldovinetti, Old, 27:209-16.
  Life of Botticelli, Old, 26:201-08.
  Life of Cimabue, Pic, 25-26.
  Life of Dello, Old, 8:62-64.
  Life of Domenico Ghirlandaio, Old, 26:201-08.
  Life of Filippino Lippi, Old, 26:201-08.
  Life of Filippo Lippi, Fra, 194-98.
  Life of Fra Bartolommeo, Pic, 1-2.
  Life of Ghiberti, Old, 26:201-08.
  Life of Giotto, Old, 35:278-80, 36:281-86.
  Life of Jacopo della Quercia, Fra, 265-69.
  Life of Leonardo da Vinci, Fra, 25-26.
  Life of Lorenzo Monaco, Old, 26:201-08 (*).
  Life of Margheritone, Old, 28:17-24.
  Life of Masaccio, Fra, 145-63, 276-80.
  Life of Michelozzo, And, 259-63 (*).

KEY TO BIBLIOGRAPHY

This bibliography supplements, revises, and corrects the entries in the Key to Bibliography in the *Compendium*, pages 503-21.

AL   Alberti, Judith Fay. "Robert Browning and Italian Renaissance Painting." Ph.D. dissertation. University of California, Berkeley, 1979.

ALB   Albrecht, Mary Louise. "The Palaces and Art Objects in 'The Statue and the Bust.'" *Studies in Browning and His Circle*, 11 (Spring 1983), 47-60.

ALL   Allott, Kenneth, ed. *Selected Poems of Robert Browning*. London: Oxford University Press, 1967.

ALT   Altick, Richard D., and James F. Loucks, II. *Browning's Roman Murder Story: A Reading of "The Ring and the Book."* Chicago: University of Chicago Press, 1968.

ARN   *Poems of Matthew Arnold.* Ed. by Kenneth Allott. 2nd edition ed. by Miriam Allott. London and New York: Longman, 1979.

BAE   *Rome and Central Italy.* Leipzig: Karl Baedeker, 1930.

BAG   Letter to the author dated October 15, 1988, from the Bagni di Lucca Terme: Azienda Autonoma di Cura e Soggiorno, Bagni di Lucca, Italy.

BAI   Letter to the author dated October 14, 1985, from D. M. Bailey, representing the Greek and Roman Antiquities Department of the British Museum, London.

BAL   Baldinucci, Filippo. *Delle notizie de'professori del disegno da Cimabue.* . . . 20 vols. Florence, 1767-1774.

BALD   —. *Notizie dei professori del disegno da Cimabue.* . . . 5 vols. Florence: V. Batelli, 1845. First published in Florence, 1681-1728.

BAN   Letter to the author dated November 11, 1976, from D. G. Banwell, of the Dulwich Picture Gallery, London.

BAR   Barfucci, Enrico. *Giornate fiorentine.* Florence: Vallecchi Editore, 1958.

BART   Bartolini, Roberto. *Florence.* Florence: Bartolini Publications, n.d.

BEC   Becci, F. *Delle Stinche di Firenze.* Florence: Le Monnier, 1839. This book may be found in the Biblioteca Marucelliana, Florence.

BED   Letter to the author dated May 18, 1978, from the Bedfordshire County Librarian, England.

BEL   Bellori, Giovanni Pietro. *Descrizzione* [sic] *delle imagini dipinte da Rafaelle* [sic] *d'Urbino nelle camere del Palazzo Apostolico Vaticano.* Roma, 1695; facsimile rpt. Farnborough, Hants: Gregg International, 1968.

BEN   Bénézit, E. *Dictionnaire critique et documentaire des peintres, sculpteurs, dessinateurs et graveurs.* 10 vols. Paris: Librairie Gründ, 1911-1923.

BER   Berdoe, Edward. *The Browning Cyclopaedia.* 2nd ed. New York: Barnes & Noble, 1958. First published in 1897.

BERE   Berenson, Bernard. *Italian Pictures of the Renaissance: Florentine School.* 2 vols. London: Phaidon, 1963.

BERM   Berman, R. J. *Browning's Duke.* New York: Richards Rosen Press, 1972.

BERT   Berti, Luciano. *Masaccio.* University Park: Pennsylvania State University Press, 1967.

BIB   *The Holy Bible.* Authorized (King James) version. Philadelphia: The National Bible Press, n.d.

BIO   *Biographie universelle.* 85 vols. Paris: Michaud Bros., 1811-1862.

BLA   Blagden, Isa. *Agnes Tremorne.* 2 vols. London: Smith, Elder, 1861.

BLO   Bloom, Harold, and Lionel Trilling, eds. *Romantic Poetry and Prose.* The Oxford Anthology of English Literature. New York: Oxford University Press, 1973.

BOA   Boas, Louise Schultz. "The Glove." *Explicator,* 2 (November 1943), item 13.

BOC   Bocchi, Francesco. *Le bellezze della città di Firenze.* Florence: n.p. (but Medici emblem is given), n.d.

BOG   Bogert, Judith. "The New Cross Knight: The Fixing of a Legend." *Studies in Browning and His Circle,* 7 (Spring 1979), 34-42.

BOL   Bolton, Frances. "Robert Browning's *Dramatic Idyls.*" Ph.D. dissertation. Yale University, 1934.

BOLZ   Letter to the author dated August 12, 1992, from the Azienda di Turismo, Bolzano, Italy.

BON   Letter to the author dated January 29, 1986, from Dr. Carla Guiducci Bonanni, director of the Biblioteca Marucelliana, Florence.

BOR   Borenius, Tancred. *Catalogue of the Pictures and Drawings at Harewood House*. Oxford: The University Press, 1936.

BRI   Bright, Michael H. "Browning's Celebrated Pictor Ignotus." *English Language Notes*, 13 (1976), 192-94, 209-15 (including reply to BULL).

BRO   *The Complete Poetic and Dramatic Works of Robert Browning*. Ed. by Horace E. Scudder. Cambridge Edition. Boston: Houghton Mifflin, 1895.

BROU   Broughton, Leslie N., and Benjamin F. Stelter. *A Concordance to the Poems of Robert Browning*. 2 vols. New York: Stechert, 1924-1925.

BROW   *Browning Society Papers*. Comp. by F. J. Furnivall. 3 vols. London: Trübner, 1881-1891.

BUL   Bullen, J. B. "Browning's 'Pictor Ignotus' and Vasari's 'Life of Fra Bartolommeo di San Marco.'" *Review of English Studies*, NS 23 (1972), 313-19.

BULL   —. "Fra Bartolommeo's Quest for Obscurity." *English Language Notes*, 13 (1976), 206-09.

BYR   Byron, George Gordon. *Complete Poetical Works of Lord Byron*. Ed. by Jerome J. McGann. 7 vols. Oxford: Clarendon Press, 1980-1993.

CAL   Calcraft, M. B. M. "'A Place to Stand and Love In': By the Refubbri Chapel with the Brownings." *Browning Society Notes*, 16 (Spring 1986), 12-22.

CAP   In conversation on August 15, 1978, with Luciano Capra, director of the Biblioteca Comunale, Ferrara, Italy.

CAR   Carrington, C. E. "My Last Duchess," *Times Literary Supplement*, November 6, 1969, p. 1288.

CARR Carr, Cornelia, ed. *Harriet Hosmer: Letters and Memories.* New York: Moffat, Yard, 1913.

CHA Champneys, Basil. *Memoirs and Correspondence of Coventry Patmore.* London: George Bell, 1900.

CHI Letter to the author dated December 6, 1979, from Dr. Marco Chiarini, Director of the Galleria Palatina di Palazzo Pitti, Florence.

CHIA Chiavacci, Egisto. *Guida della Galleria del Palazzo Pitti.* 2nd ed. Florence: M. Cellini, 1862. The annotation reads as it does below under DOM.

COL *Complete Poetical Works of Samuel Taylor Coleridge.* Ed. by E. Hartley Coleridge. 2 vols. Oxford: Clarendon Press, 1912.

CON Conroy, Marilyn Ann. "Browning's Use of Art Objects." Ph.D. dissertation. Indiana University, 1971.

COO Cook, Eleanor. "Browning's 'Bellori.'" *Notes and Queries* (September 1970), 334-35.

COOK Cook, A. K. *A Commentary upon Browning's "The Ring and the Book."* Hamden, Conn.: Archon Books, 1966. First published in 1920.

COOKE Cooke, George Willis. *A Guide-Book to the Poetic and Dramatic Works of Robert Browning.* Boston: Houghton Mifflin, 1891.

COR Corson, Hiram. *An Introduction to the Study of Robert Browning's Poetry.* Boston: Heath, 1903.

CRI Letter to the author dated July 2, 1981, from Miss. C. Crichton-Stuart, Secretary to the Surveyor of the Queen's Pictures, Lord Chamberlain's Office, St. James's Palace, London.

CRO Crowder, Ashby Bland, Jr. "Browning's *The Inn Album.*" Ph.D. dissertation. University of London, 1972.

CROW   —. "The Inn Album: A Record of 1875." *Browning Institute Studies*, 2 (1974), 43-64.

CROWE   Crowe, Sir Joseph Archer, and Giovanni Battista Cavalcaselle. *A New History of Painting in Italy: from the II to the XVI Century.* Ed. by Edward Hutton. 3 vols. London: Dent, 1908-1909. First published in 1864.

DAH   Dahl, Curtis. "Browning, Architecture, and John Ruskin." *Studies in Browning and His Circle*, 6 (Spring 1978), 32-45.

DAR   Letters to the author dated March 25 and August 1, 1983, from Dr. Alan P. Darr, Curator in Charge of European Sculpture and Decorative Arts, The Detroit Institute of Arts.

DAV   Davies, F. "Browning's 'The Guardian Angel.'" *Times Literary Supplement*, 32, 1933, p. 692.

DAVI   Davies, Martin. *National Gallery Catalogue: The Earlier Italian Schools.* 2nd ed. London: National Gallery, 1961.

DE   DeVane, William Clyde. "The Landscape of Browning's 'Childe Roland.'" *PMLA*, 11 (1925), 426-32.

DEL   DeLaura, David J. "The Context of Browning's Painter Poems: Aesthetics, Polemics, Historics." *PMLA*, 95 (May 1980), 367-88.

DELA   —. "Some Notes on Browning's Pictures and Painters." *Studies in Browning and His Circle*, 8 (Fall 1980), 7-16.

DELAU   —. "Ruskin, Arnold and Browning's Grammarian: 'Crowded with Culture.'" *In Victorian Perspectives.* Ed. by John Clubbe and Jerome Meckier. New York: Macmillan, 1989, pp. 68-119.

     Special appreciation is extended to David De-

Laura, Professor of English and former Chairman of the English Department at the University of Pennsylvania. Professor DeLaura's encouragement and assistance over the years has culminated in his contributions to and critique of the *Compendium* and this appendix. His detailed attention to matters of form has been superior, and his insights into content have been exceptional. Contributions by Professor DeLaura of both source work and analysis are entered under And, 103-12 (*Comp.*, 26-28); Fra, 145-63 (*Comp.*, 110-11), 183-93 (*Comp.*, 426-27), 286-90 (*Comp.*, 427), 344-81 (*Comp.*, 429); Gra, 13-16, 31-34 (*App. A*); Old, 24:185-92, 27:209-16 (*Comp.*, 193, 194, 195, 196); and Pic, 1-2 (*Comp.*, 228), 38-41 (*Comp.*, 229).

DEV   DeVane, William Clyde. *A Browning Handbook.* 1st ed. New York: F. S. Crofts, 1935.

DEVA   —. *A Browning Handbook.* 2nd ed. Appleton-Century-Crofts, 1955.

DEVAN   —. *Browning's Parleyings: The Autobiography of a Mind.* New York: Russell & Russell, 1964. First published in 1927.

DEVANE   —. "The Virgin and the Dragon." *Yale Review,* 37 (September 1947), 33-46.

DIZ   Bordenache Battaglia, Gabriella. "Castellani." In the *Dizionario biografico degli italiani.* Vol. 21, July 1972, pp. 590-605.

DO   Dooley, Allan C. "Another Detail from Vasari in 'Fra Lippo Lippi.'" *Studies in Browning and His Circle,* 5 (Spring 1977), 51.

DOO   —. "Browning's *Prince Hohenstiel-Schwangau*: An Annotated Edition with an Introductory Study of Napoleon III in Victorian Literature." Ph.D. dissertation. Northwestern University, 1970.

DOOL   —. "Andrea, Raphael, and the Moment of 'Andrea del Sarto.'" *Modern Philology, 81* (August 1983), 38-46.

DOM   Domenico Gazzadi da Sassuolo. "Andrea del Sarto: i due ritratti ambidue di sua mano." In *L'imperiale e reale galleria Pitti.*" Ed. by Luigi Bardi. Florence: coi tipi della Galileliana, 1837, 1: no page number. The annotation reads in the original as follows:

> Sembra questo quadro alludere al passo doloroso della vita d'Andrea. Quando invitato per lettere da Francesco I a ritornare in Francia, gli fu della moglie impedito.

DOU   Douglas, Norman. *Siren Land and Fountains in the Sand.* London: Secker and Warburg, 1957.

DUF   Duffin, Henry Charles. *Amphibian: A Reconsideration of Browning.* London: Bowes & Bowes, 1956.

DUL   *Catalogue of the Pictures in the Gallery of Alleyn's College of God's Gifts at Dulwich.* Revised in 1914 by Sir Edward Cook. By order of the Governors, 1926 (n.p.).

DULW   *A Brief Catalogue of the Pictures in Dulwich College Picture Gallery.* By order of the Governors, 1953 (n.p).

DUP   Dupras, Joseph A. "'An Epistle. . . of Karshish' and Froment's *Lazarus Triptych*: The Uffizi Connection." *Studies in Browning and His Circle,* 9 (Fall 1981), 50-56.

DUS   Dussler, Luitpold. *Raphael: A Critical Catalogue of His Pictures, Wall-paintings, and Tapestries.* London: Phaidon, 1971.

EGG   Egg, Erich. *Das Grabmal Kaiser Maximilians I: Hofkirche in Innsbruck.* Innsbruck: Kunstverlag Hofstetter, 1988.

EIS   Eisenberg, Marvin. "'The Penitent St. Jerome' by
             Giovanni Toscani." *The Burlington Magazine*, 118
             (May 1976), 274-83.

EISE   —. Correspondence to the author between 1983-
             1994 from Professor Marvin Eisenberg, of the De-
             partment of the History of Art, University of
             Michigan.
             Special appreciation is expressed to Professor
             Eisenberg, who, as one of the readers listed in the
             prefaces of this study, has gone far beyond the task
             of reading the manuscript and proofs for correct-
             ness, precision, and clarity, as important as these
             matters are. He has also systematized the form of
             the captions for the illustrations, standardized the
             foreign terms and names, resolved research prob-
             lems with pertinent documentation, and, most
             important, contributed numerous original source
             possibilities. The bulk of Professor Eisenberg's con-
             tributions, both original and auxiliary, are listed in
             this work under And, 259-63 (*Comp.*, 420; *App. A*);
             Bi, 666-68 (*Comp.*, 422); Bis, 56-60 (*Comp.*, 423); Cle,
             82, 88-94 (*App. A*); Fra, 70-75, 189-90, 265-69, 323-32,
             344-81 (*Comp.*, 102, 111, 118, 121, 429); My, 54-56
             (*Comp.*, 177); Old, 201-08 (*Comp.*, 195; *App. A*); Pic,
             25-26, 31-33 (*Comp.*, 229); and Rin, I.1-4, 15-17
             (*Comp.*, 440; *App. A*), I.38-52 (*Comp.*, 441-42; *App.
             A*); IV.320-25 (*Comp.*, 443); VI.400-06, 1249-55
             (*Comp.*, 306, 444; *App. A*); and IX.26-27, 120-30
             (*Comp.*, 447). Also, see under the Index of Sources
             with Locations, *App. A*, Varallo, Italy.

EISEN   —. *Lorenzo Monaco*. Princeton: Princeton Univer-
             sity Press, 1989.

EISS   Eissenstat, Martha Turnquist. "Robert Browning's
             Use of Italian Renaissance Sources." Ph.D. disserta-
             tion. University of Kansas, 1968.

ELI   *Elizabeth Barrett Browning: Letters to Her Sister,
             1847-1859.* Ed. by Leonard Huxley. New York: Dut-
             ton, 1930.

ESP This information was obtained through interviews in early June, 1982, with Antonio D'Esposito, Parroco of the Santissima Trinità, in Piano di Sorrento, and former Parroco Don Antonino Alberino, of the same church. For further documentation concerning the connection between the Dominican order and the Feast of the Madonna of the Rosary, inquire into letters from Dominican priests in the archives of the Church of the Santissima Trinità and consult Pasquale Ferraivolo's *Chiese e monasteri di Sorrento: cenni storici ed artistici*, ed. by the Congregation of the Servi di Maria, Sorrento, 1974, pp. 110-13.

FAL Faldi, Italo. *Pittori viterbesi di cinque secoli*. Rome: Ugo Bozzi Roma, 1970.

FOW Fowler, Rowena. "Browning's Nudes." *Victorian Poetry*, 27 (Autumn-Winter 1989), 29-47.

FRE Freedberg, S. J. *Andrea del Sarto: Catalogue Raisonné*. 2 vols. Cambridge, Mass.: Harvard University Press, 1963.

FRI Friedland, Louis S. "Ferrara and 'My Last Duchess.'" *Studies in Philology*, 33 (1936), 656-84.

GERK Letter to the author dated June 7, 1982, from Dr. Gerhard Gerkins, director of the Kunsthalle, Bremen, Germany.

GIB Gibson, Mary Ellis. "The Poetry of Struggle: Browning's Style and 'The Parleying with Gerard de Lairesse.'" *Victorian Poetry*, 19 (Autumn 1981), 225-42.

GIP *La Gipsoteca di Possagno*. Elena Bassi, ed. Venice: Neri Pozza Editore, 1957.

GRE Greenberg, Robert A. "Ruskin, Pugin, and the Contemporary Context of 'The Bishop Orders His Tomb.'" *PMLA*, 84 (1969), 1588-94.

GRI   Griffin, W. H., and H. C. Minchin. *The Life of Robert Browning.* Hamden, Conn.: Archon, 1966. First published in 1910.

GRID   Gridley, Roy E. *The Brownings and France: A Chronicle with Commentary.* London: The Athlone Press, 1982.

GRIF   Griffo, Mary Ann. "Robert Browning and the Sister Arts." Ph.D. dissertation. University of California, Riverside, 1983.

GRIFF   Griffith, George V. "'Andrea del Sarto' and the New Jerusalem." *Victorian Poetry*, 15 (Winter 1977), 371-72.

GUI   *Les guides bleus, Paris.* Paris: Librairie Hachette, 1952.

HA   Hardy, Florence Emily. *The Early Life of Thomas Hardy, 1840-1891.* New York: Macmillan, 1928.

HAL   Hall, James. *Dictionary of Subjects and Symbols in Art.* New York: Harper & Row, 1974.

HAR   Hare, Augustus J. C. *Florence.* London: George Routledge and Sons, n.d.

HARE   —. *Walks in Rome.* 2 vols. London: George Allen, 1903.

HARP   Harper, J. W., ed. *Men and Women, and Other Poems.* London: J. M. Dent, 1975.

HARR   Harrington, Vernon C. *Browning Studies.* Boston: Richard G. Badger, 1915.

HAWL   Hawlin, Stefin. "Browning's 'A Toccata of Galuppi's': How Venice Once Was Dear." *Review of English Studies*, 41, No. 164 (1990), 496-509.

HAWT   Hawthorne, Nathaniel. *The Complete Novels and Selected Tales of Nathaniel Hawthorne.* Ed. by Norman Holmes Pearson. New York: The Modern Library, 1937.

HAZ   Hazlitt, William. *Sketches of the Principal Picture-Galleries in England.* London: Taylor and Hessey, 1824.

HAZL   —. *The Complete Works of William Hazlitt.* Ed. by P. Howe. 21 vols. London and Toronto: J.M.Dent, 1933. "Flaxman's Lectures on Sculpture" first appeared in *The Edinburgh Review,* 50 (October 1829).

HE   Herbert, George. *The Works of George Herbert.* Ed. by F. E. Hutchinson. Oxford: Clarendon, 1964.

HER   Herford, C. H. *Robert Browning.* New York: Dodd, Mead, 1905.

HIL   *Portraits by Sir Joshua Reynolds.* Ed. by Frederick W. Hilles. New York: McGraw-Hill, 1952.

HOD   Hodell, Charles W., ed. and tr. *The Old Yellow Book: Source of Robert Browning's "The Ring and the Book. . . ."* 2nd ed. Washington, DC: Carnegie Institute of Washington, 1916.

HOO   Hood, Thurmond L., ed. *Letters of Robert Browning, Collected by Thomas J. Wise.* New Haven: Yale University Press, 1933.

HUM   Letter to the author dated July 15, 1985, from Dr. N. Humburg, Director of the Museum Hameln, Hamelin, Germany.

IRV   Irvine, William, and Park Honan. *The Book, the Ring, and the Poet.* New York: McGraw-Hill, 1974.

IST   The archives are at the Istituto Germanico di Storia dell'Arte, in Florence. The books dealing with the façade of the Duomo are as follows: Luigi del Moro, *Facciata di S. Maria del Fiore* (Florence: Giuseppe Ferroni, 1888); Walter and Elizabeth Paatz, *Die Kirchen von Florenz* (Frankfurt: Vol. III, Vittorio Klostermann, 1952), pp. 320ff; and Voti and Pareri, et al, *Sulla facciata del Duomo* (Florence: M. Cellini, 1865). The Paatz volume contains an extensive bibliography and specifically locates the designs today.

JAC   Jack, Ian. *Browning's Major Poetry.* Oxford: Clarendon Press, 1973.

JACK   Jack, Ian, Rowena Fowler, and Margaret Smith, eds. *The Poetical Works of Robert Browning.* Vols. 1-4. Oxford: Clarendon Press, 1983-1991.

JAM   James, Henry. *William Wetmore Story and His Friends.* 2 vols. Boston: Houghton Mifflin, 1903.

JAME   Jameson, Mrs. Anna. *Sacred and Legendary Art.* 2 vols. London: Longmans, Green, and Co., 1870. First published in London in 1848.

JAMES   —. *Sketches of Art, Literature, and Character.* Boston: Ticknor and Fields, 1847. First published in London as *Art, Literature, and Social Morals.*

JAMESO   —. *Legends of the Madonna.* In *The Writings of Anna Jameson.* 5 vols. Boston: Houghton Mifflin, 1897. First printed in 1852.

JER   Jerrold, Blanchard. *Life of Gustave Doré.* London: H. W. Allen, 1891.

KEA   Keats, John. *Complete Poems.* Ed. by Jack Stillinger. Cambridge, Mass: Belknap Press, 1982.

KEL   Kelley, Philip, and Betty A. Coley. *The Browning Collections: A Reconstruction with Other Memorabilia.* Winfield, Kansas: Wedgestone Press, 1984.

KELL   Kelley, Philip, and Ronald Hudson. *The Brown-
            ings' Correspondence: A Checklist*. New York/
            Winfield: The Browning Institute and Wedgestone
            Press, 1978.

KELLE   Kelley, Philip, Betty A. Coley, and Richard Town-
            send. "The Paintings, Sculpture and Drawings of
            Robert Wiedemann Barrett Browning (1849-1912):
            A Catalogue Raisonné." *Studies in Browning and
            His Circle*, 10 (Spring 1982), 7-35.

KEN   *The Letters of Elizabeth Barrett Browning*. Ed. by
            Frederic G. Kenyon. 2 vols. New York: Macmillan,
            1897.

KENE   Kennedy, Richard S. *Robert Browning's "Asolan-
            do": The Indian Summer of a Poet*. Columbia: Uni-
            versity of Missouri Press, 1993.

KI   Kincaid, A. N. "The Ring and the Scholars."
            Browning Institute Studies, 8 (1980), 151-59.

KIN   *The Letters of Robert Browning and Elizabeth Bar-
            rett Barrett, 1845-46*. Ed. by Elvan Kintner. 2 vols.
            Cambridge, Mass.: Belknap Press, 1969.

KING   King, Roma A., Jr., et al, eds. *The Complete Works
            of Robert Browning*. Vols. 1-5, 7-9. Athens, Ohio:
            Ohio University Press, Baylor University, 1969-1989.

KNI   Knickerbocker, Kenneth Leslie. "A Critical Analy-
            sis of Robert Browning's *Pacchiarotto* Volume with
            a Study of the Background (1867-1876)." Ph.D. dis-
            sertation. Yale University, 1933.

KNIG   Knight, Charles, ed. *London*. 6 vols. London: H. G.
            Bohn, 1861.

KO   Korg, Jacob. *Browning and Italy*. Athens, Ohio:
            Ohio University Press, 1983.

KOR   —. "Browning's Art and 'By the Fireside.'" *Victorian Poetry*, 15 (Summer 1977), 147-58.

KRY   Krynicky, Harry Thomas. "*Christmas-Eve and Easter-Day* by Robert Browning: A Variorum Text." Ph.D. dissertation. University of Pennsylvania, 1974.

LAI   Lairesse, Gerard de. *The Art of Painting in All Its Branches*. . . . Tr. by John Frederick Fritsch. London: S. Vandenbergh, 1778.

LAN   Langbaum, Robert. "Browning and the Question of Myth." In *Robert Browning: A Collection of Critical Essays*. Ed. by Harold Bloom and Adrienne Munich. Englewood Cliffs, New Jersey: Prentice-Hall, 1979, pp. 148-66.

LEI   Leisgang, Waltraud. "'Fra Lippo Lippi': A Picture Poem." *Browning Society Notes*, 3 (December 1973), 20-32.

LEV   Levi, Karen, ed. *The Power of Love: Six Centuries of Diamond Betrothal Rings*. London: Diamond Information Center, 1988.

LIN   Lindsay, J. D. "The Central Episode in Browning's 'By the Fireside.'" *Studies in Philology*, 39 (1942), 571-79.

LIT   Litzinger, Boyd. "Robert Browning and the Babylonian Woman." *Baylor Browning Interests*, 19 (May 1962), 5-35.

LUC   Letter to the author dated March 15, 1979, from the Soprintendenza per i beni ambientali, architettonici, artistici e storici per le province di Pisa, Livorno, Lucca, e Massa Carrara, Pisa, Italy.

MA   Marabottini, Alessandro. *Polidoro da Caravaggio*. 2 vols. Rome: Edizioni dell'Elefante, 1969.

MAC   Mackendrick, Paul. *The Greek Stones Speak.* New York: St. Martin's Press, 1962.

MAJ   Major, Mabel. "Robert Browning and the Florentine Renaissance." *Texas Christian University Quarterly*, 1 (July 1924), 5-74.

MAR   Marchini, Giuseppe. *Filippo Lippi.* Milan: Electa Editrice, 1975.

MARK   Markus, Julia. "Browning's 'Andrea' Letter at Wellesley College: A Correction of DeVane's *Handbook.*" *Studies in Browning and His Circle*, 1 (Fall 1973), 52-55.

MARKUS   —. "'Old Pictures in Florence' Through *Casa Guidi Windows.*" *Browning Institute Studies*, 6 (1978), 43-61.

MART   Martin, Gregory. *Catalogue of the Flemish School, 1600-1900.* London: National Gallery, n.d.

MARTI   Martindale, Andrew, and Edi Baccheschi. *The Complete Works of Giotto.* New York: Abrams, 1966.

MCA   McAleer, Edward C., ed. *Dearest Isa: Robert Browning's Letters to Isabella Blagden.* Austin: University of Texas Press, 1951.

MCAL   —, ed. *Learned Lady: Letters from Robert Browning to Mrs. Thomas Fitzgerald, 1876-1889.* Cambridge: Harvard University Press, 1966.

MEL   Melchiori, Barbara. "Where the Bishop Orders His Tomb." *Review of English Literature*, 5 (1964), 7-26. Also published in Melchiori's *Browning's Poetry of Reticence* (New York: Barnes & Noble, 1968), pp. 20-39.

MELC   —. "Browning's *Don Juan.*" In *Browning's Poetry of Reticence.* New York: Barnes & Noble, 1968, pp. 158-87.

MER   Meredith, Michael. *Meeting the Brownings*. Waco, Texas: Armstrong Browning Library, Baylor University, 1986.

MERE   Meredith, Michael, and Rita S. Humphrey, eds. *More Than Friend: The Letters of Robert Browning to Katherine de Kay Bronson*. Waco, Texas, and Winfield, Kansas: Armstrong Browning Library and Wedgestone Press, 1985.

MES   Letter to the author dated June 22, 1982, from Professor Fede Messedaglia, of the Comune di Goito, Province of Mantua, Italy.

MI   *Michelin Italy*. Rennes, France: Ouest-Impression, 1989.

MIC   *Michelin Benelux*. Paris: Services de Tourisme, 1972.

MICH   *Michelin Italy*. 6th ed. London: The Dickens Press, 1966.

MIL   Miller, Betty. *Robert Browning, A Portrait*. London: John Murray, 1952.

MILL   Letter to the author dated November 25, 1982, from Dr. Albrecht Miller, director of the Bayerische Verwaltung der Staatlichen Schlösser, Gärten und Seen, Munich.

MILT   Milton, John. *John Milton: Complete Poems and Major Prose*. Ed. by Merritt Y. Hughes. Indianapolis: Dobbs-Merrill, 1957.

MU   Munich, Adrienne Auslander. "Emblems of Temporality in Browning's 'Cleon.'" *Browning Institute Studies*, 6 (1978), 117-36.

MUR   *Handbook for Travellers in Central Italy*. London: John Murray, 1843.

MURR   *Russia*. London: John Murray, 1893.

MURRA   *Handbook for Travellers in Switzerland and the Alps of Savoy and Piedmont.* London: John Murray, 1828.

MURRAY   *Handbook for Travellers in Northern Italy.* London: John Murray, 1846.

NA   Letter to the author dated November 9, 1979, from the Archives du Département et du Comte Nantais, Nantes, Loire-Atlantique, France.

NE   *New Poems of Robert Browning and Elizabeth Barrett Browning.* Ed. by Sir Frederic G. Kenyon. New York: Macmillan, 1915.

NEW   *New Letters of Robert Browning.* Ed. by William C. DeVane and Kenneth L. Knickerbocker. New Haven: Yale University Press, 1950.

NEY   Ney, Marie. "Was It a Procession of the Service Order in 'Down in the City'? a Query." *Browning Society Newsletter*, 5 (March 1975), 27.

OFF   Letter to the author dated August 10, 1979, from the librarian of the Offentliche Bibliothek, Aachen, Germany.

OG   *Elizabeth Barrett Browning's Letters to Mrs. David Ogilvy, 1849-1861.* Ed. by Peter N. Heydon and Philip Kelley. New York: Quadrangle/The Browning Institute, 1973.

ON   D'Onofrio, Cesare. *Le Fontane di Roma.* Rome: Staderin Editore, 1957.

OR   Orr, Mrs. Sutherland. *A Handbook to the Works of Robert Browning.* London: G. Bell and Sons, 1937. First published in 1885.

ORM   Ormond, Leonée. "Browning and Painting." In *Robert Browning*. Ed. by Isobel Armstrong. Athens, Ohio: Ohio University Press, 1974, pp. 184-210.

ORMO   Ormond, Leonée and Richard. *Lord Leighton*. New Haven: Yale University Press, 1975.

ORMON   Letter to the author dated September 10, 1983, from Leonée Ormond, of King's College, London.

ORMOND Ormond, Richard. *Early Victorian Portraits*. 2 vols. London: HMSO, 1973.

ORR   Orr, Mrs. Sutherland. *Life and Letters of Robert Browning*. Ed. by F. G. Kenyon. 2nd ed. London: Smith, Elder, 1908. First published in 1891.

PAR   Parr, Johnstone. "Browning's 'Fra Lippo Lippi,' Baldinucci, and the Milanesi Edition of Vasari." *English Language Notes*, 3 (March 1966), 197-201.

PARR   —. "Browning's 'Fra Lippo Lippi,' Vasari's Masaccio, and Mrs. Jameson." *English Language Notes*, 5 (June 1968), 277-83.

PAS   Pasqui, V. *Guida d'Arezzo*. Arezzo: Società Tipografica Aretina, 1925.

PET   Pettigrew, John, and Thomas J. Collins, eds. *Robert Browning: The Poems*. 2 vols. New Haven: Yale University Press, 1981.

PIL   Pilkington, The Rev. M. *A Dictionary of Painters, from the Revival of the Art to the Present Period*. Ed. by Henry Fuseli. London: John Crowder, 1805.

POR   Porter, Charlotte, and Helen A. Clarke. *The Complete Works of Robert Browning*. 12 vols. New York: Thomas Crowell, 1898.

POU			Pouncey, Philip, and J. A. Gere. *Italian Drawings in the Department of Prints and Drawings in the British Museum: Raphael and His Circle.* London: British Museum, 1962.

PRA			Praeger, Robert Lloyd. *Official Guide to Co. Down.* Belfast: Belfast and Co. Down Railway, 1900.

PRO			Procacci, Ugo. *La Casa Buonarroti a Firenze.* N.p.: Electa Milano, 1965.

QUA			Quarles, Francis. *Emblems, Divine and Moral.* London: Milton Press, 1839.

RAD			Radford, Ernest. "The Moorish Front to the Duomo in 'Luria.'" *Browning Society Papers,* 2 (1881-1884), 251-52. In a footnote on p. 251 the description of the design for the façade reads:

> Progetto per la facciata della Metropolitana di Firenze composto e disegnato nel 1822 dall'Architetto Giovanni Silvestri ed inviato all' I. R. Accademia delle Belle Arti. —Giovanni Silvestri e Felice Francolini Architetti dedicano al loro concittadini. 1833.

RAY			Raymond, William O. "Browning's Dark Mood: A Study of *Fifine at the Fair.*" *Studies in Philology,* 31 (1934), 578-99; also in *The Infinite Moment and Other Essays in Robert Browning.* Toronto: University of Toronto Press, 1950, pp. 105-28.

RIC			Richter, Gisela. *The Sculpture and Sculptors of the Greeks.* New Haven: Yale University Press, 1970.

RIG			Letters to the author dated October 31, 1978, and April 4, 1981, from Dr. Fernando Rigon, Director of the Museo, Biblioteca, e Archivio di Bassano del Grappa, Bassano del Grappa, Italy.

RIO			Rio, Alexis-François. *The Poetry of Christian Art.* Tr. by Miss Wells. London: Bosworth, 1854.

RIZ			*Rizzoli Classici dell'arte: Canova #85.* N.p., n.d.

ROL   Rolfe, William J., and Heloise E. Hersey, eds. *Select Poems of Robert Browning*. New York: American Book Co., 1886.

ROM   Letters to the author dated January 1 and September 5, 1983, from Giandomenico Romanelli, Director of the Civic Museums of Art and History in Venice.

RUS   *The Works of John Ruskin*. Ed. by E. T. Cook and Alexander Wedderburn. 39 vols. London: George Allen, 1903-1912.

RYA   Ryals, Clyde de L. *Browning's Later Poetry, 1871-1889*. Ithaca: Cornell University Press, 1975.

RYAL   —. "Browning's *Fifine at the Fair*: Some Further Sources and Influences." *English Language Notes*, 7 (September 1969), 46-51.

SAM   Letters to the author dated August 9, 1976, and September 15, 1977, from Jean-Pierre Samoyault, Conservateur du Musée National du Château de Fontainebleau, France.

SAN   Letter to the author dated January 9, 1980, from Bettini Santo, parish priest of Santa Maria a Olmi e Sant'Ansano, Borgo di San Lorenzo, Italy.

SC   Schweik, Robert C. "Bishop Blougram's Miracles." *Modern Language Notes*, 71 (June 1956), 416-18.

SCO   Scott, Sir Walter. *The Poetical Works of Sir Walter Scott*. Ed. by J. Logie Robertson. London: Oxford University Press, 1960.

SH   Shearman, John. *Andrea del Sarto*. 2 vols. Oxford: Clarendon Press, 1965.

SHA   *The Riverside Shakespeare*. Ed. by G. Blakemore Evans et al. Boston: Houghton Mifflin, 1974.

SHE Shelley, Percy Bysshe. *Complete Works of Percy Bysshe Shelley.* Ed. by Roger Ingpen and Walter E. Peck. 10 vols. London: E. Benn, 1926-1930.

SIE Lusini, Aldo, and Sandro Chierichetti. *Siena: An Illustrated Guide-Book.* 4th ed. Siena: Stefano Venturini, 1966.

SIR Sirugo, Marilyn S. "The Site of 'Love Among the Ruins' Revisited." *Studies in Browning and His Circle*, 4 (Spring 1976), 41-48.

SMI Smith, Arthur Hamilton. *A Guide to the Collection of Casts of Sculpture in the Department of Greek and Roman Antiquities in the British Museum.* London: By Order of the Trustees, 1913.

SOS Letter to the author dated August 14, 1978, from Dr. Piero Sospecchi, attaché to the Pinacoteca, Siena.

SOT Sotheby, Wilkinson, and Hodge. *The Browning Collections.* London: The Dryden Press, 1913.

SOTH *Sotheran's Price Current of Literature: Illustrated Catalogue.* Vol. 757. London: Sotheran, 1913.

SOU Southwell, Samuel B. *Quest for Eros: Browning and 'Fifine.'* Lexington: The University Press of Kentucky, 1980.

SPO In consultation on August 17, 1972, with Father Pierdamiano Sportono, Curator of the Vallombrosan Monastery, Vallombrosa, Italy.

STE Stevens, L. Robert. "'My Last Duchess': A Possible Source." *Victorian Newsletter*, 28 (Fall 1965), 25-26.

STEV Stevenson, Lionel. "The Pertinacious Victorian Poets. In *Victorian Literature: Modern Essays in Criticism.* Ed. by Austin Wright. New York: Oxford University Press, 1961, pp. 16-31.

STU   Stubblebine, James H. *Duccio di Buoninsegna and His School.* 2 vols. Princeton: Princeton University Press, 1979.

TAP   Taplin, Gardner B. *The Life of Elizabeth Barrett Browning.* New Haven: Yale University Press, 1957.

TAY   Taylor, Gerald, ed. *Finger Rings: From Ancient Egypt to the Present.* London: Lund Humphries, 1978.

TEN   Tennyson, Alfred, Lord. *The Poems of Tennyson.* Ed. by Christopher Ricks. 3 vols. 2nd ed. Berkeley: University of California Press, 1987.

TER   Terreni, Jacopo and Antonio. *Viaggio pittorico della Toscana.* Vol. I. Florence: Giuseppe Tofani, 1801.

THI   Thieme, Ulrich, and Felix Becker. *Allgemeines Lexikon der bildenden Künstler.* . . . 37 vols. Leipzig: Verlag von E. A. Seemann, 1908-1950.

THO   Thomas, Charles Flint (formerly Charles Lynde-Flint Waterman). "The Painting of St. Laurence in 'Fra Lippo Lippi': Its Source at Prato." *Studies in Browning and His Circle,* 6 (Fall 1978), 45-51. (KO, p. 114, p. 229, n. 10, p. 242, refers to this article and mistakenly identifies the author as "Charles Thomas Flint.")

THOM   —. "The Setting for 'Bishop Blougram's Apology': St. George's Cathedral, Southwark." *Studies in Browning and His Circle,* 5 (Spring 1977), 27-33.

THOMA   —. "The Browning Busts at the South London Art Gallery." *Studies in Browning and His Circle,* 3 (Spring 1975), 50-51, 96-101. This article provides background for the bust of Robert Browning, by Henry Charles Fehr, that is used as the Frontispiece for the *Compendium,* and the bust of Elizabeth Barrett Browning, by Henry Alfred Pegram, that is employed as the Frontispiece in this appendix.

THOMAS —. "Robert Browning's Poetic Art Objects: An Illustrated Compendium." Ph.D. dissertation. Baylor University, 1979.

THOMAS[1] —. "Real Sources for the Bishop's Tomb in the Church of St. Praxed." *Studies in Browning and His Circle*, 12 (Spring-Fall 1984), 160-64. (WOO, II, p. 259, p. 268, l. 60n, refers to this article and mistakenly identifies the author of it as "J. W. Binns.")

THOMAS[2] —. *Art and Architecture in the Poetry of Robert Browning: An Illustrated Compendium of Sources.* Troy, New York: Whitston, 1991. Referred to in this appendix as the *Compendium (Comp.)*.

TIM Timbs, John. *Curiosities of London.* London: John Camden Hotten, 1855.

TON Letter to the author dated August 13, 1974, from Dr. Giorgio Tononi, director of the Azienda Autonoma Turismo, Trent.

TRE Treves, Sir Frederick. *The Country of "The Ring and the Book."* London: Cassell, 1913.

TUR Turner, Paul, ed. *Browning: "Men and Women."* London: Oxford University Press, 1972.

UFF *Nuovo catalogo dell'Imperiale e Reale Galleria di Firenze, 1851.* Florence: Tipografia Soliani, 1851.

V A Vasari, Giorgio. *Le Vite de'più eccellenti pittori, scultori, e architettori.* Ed. by Gaetano Milanesi, Carlo Milanesi, Carlo Pini, Padre Vincenzo Marchese. 13 vols. Florence: Felice le Monnier, 1846-1857. (Vol. XIV added in 1870). The copy that Browning had in his library is now owned by the Sotheran Co., London.

VAS   —. *Lives of Seventy of the Most Eminent Painters, Sculptors, and Architects.* 4 vols. Ed. by E. H. and E. W. Blashfield and A. A. Hopkins. Tr. by Mrs. Jonathan Foster. New York: Charles Scribner, 1897.

VASA   —. *Lives of Seventy of the Most Eminent Painters, Sculptors, and Architects.* Tr. by Mrs. Jonathan Foster. 5 vols. London: Henry G. Bohn, 1850-1864. (Vol. VI, a commentary by J. P. Richter, added in 1865).

VASAR   —. *Lives of the Most Eminent Painters, Sculptors, and Architects.* Tr. by Gaston du C. De Vere. 10 vols. London: Macmillan and the Medici Society, 1912-1915.

VASARI   —. *Le Vite de'più eccellenti architettori, pittori, e scultori italiani.* . . . Florence: 1550. 3 vols. in 2. The copy that Browning owned is in the rare book section of the Paley Library in Temple University, Philadelphia.

VAU   Vaughan, Herbert. *Florence and Her Treasures.* New York: Macmillan, 1911.

WAR   Ward, Maisie. *The Tragi-Comedy of Pen Browning.* With an introduction by Robert Coles, M.D. New York: Sheed and Ward and The Browning Institute, 1972.

WEB   Webber, F. R. *Church Symbolism.* Intr. by Ralph Adams Cram. 2nd ed. Cleveland: J. H. Jansen, 1938.

WET   Wethey, Harold Edwin. *The Paintings of Titian.* 3 vols. London: Phaidon, 1969-1975.

WH   White, John. *Duccio: Tuscan Art and the Medieval Workshop.* London: Thames and Hudson, 1979.

WHI   Whiting, Lilian. *The Brownings: Their Life and Art.* Boston: Little, Brown, 1911.

WHIT   Whitla, William. "Browning and the Ashburton Affair." *Browning Society Notes*, 2 (July 1972), 12-41.

WIT   Withers, Sara, and Samuel. "The Palazzo in 'The Statue and the Bust.'" *Browning Newsletter*, 8 (Spring 1972), 45-46.

WOO   Woolford, John, and Daniel Karlin, eds. *The Poems of Browning*. Vols. 1 and 2. London: Longman, 1991.

WOR   Worsfold, Basil, ed. *Browning's "Men and Women."* 2 vols. London: Chatto and Windus, 1907.

WORD   Wordsworth, William. *The Poetical Works of William Wordsworth*. Ed. by E. De Selincort and H. Darbishire. 2nd ed. Oxford: Clarendon Press, 1954.